28/10/23

The
CBT
Workbook

Dr Stephanie Fitzgerald

Dedicated to James Brooklyn Jay & Maurice Fitzgerald

The
CBT
Workbook

Dr Stephanie Fitzgerald

First published in Great Britain in 2013 by Hodder & Stoughton. An Hachette UK company.

First published in US in 2013 by The McGraw-Hill Companies, Inc.

Cover image © Sergiy Serdyuk – Fotolia

Typeset by Cenveo® Publisher Services.

Printed and bound by CPI Group (UK) Ltd, Croydon, CR0 4YY.

Hodder & Stoughton policy is to use papers that are natural, renewable and recyclable products and made from wood grown in sustainable forests. The logging and manufacturing processes are expected to conform to the environmental regulations of the country of origin.

Hodder & Stoughton Ltd

338 Euston Road

London NW1 3BH

www.hodder.co.uk

Acknowledgments

I would like to express my thanks to Victoria Roddam, Sam Richardson and Sarah Stubbs at Hodder & Stoughton for asking me to write this book and for their help and guidance throughout the process. I would also like to thank my family and friends who mean the world to me.

Above all I would like to thank my patients, without whom I wouldn't have had any of my wonderful experiences. It is an honour to work with them all, doing the job I love, and I thank them for letting me be part of their journey.

Contents

How to use this workbook

→ What is this book about?

The CBT Workbook is designed to provide a practical introduction to the key principles and ideas behind Cognitive Behavioural Therapy (CBT). The style of the workbook means that you can read about, and then practise, some core techniques. Through completing short exercises and answering questions, you can begin to explore where CBT techniques will help you, and monitor the impact of the changes you make in your life.

WHAT'S DIFFERENT ABOUT THIS BOOK?

By incorporating the practical exercises, this workbook takes you beyond the theory and allows you to practise the techniques and see the results for yourself. If you are new to CBT, or are considering therapy and want to have a clearer idea of what that involves, then this book is perfect for you.

Unlike other books on CBT, this book also considers those around you. Chapter 13 talks you through how to explain any changes you make to other people, as well as how to maintain these in situations others may make more difficult for you. Additionally, this book provides some help and support for those around you. The chapter for friends, family and carers is designed to help others make sense of what is going on for you and know how best to support and help you.

WHAT CAN I EXPECT?

This book focuses on the following areas:

▶ identifying your problem(s)

▶ setting goals to overcome these and achieve what you want

▶ identifying and challenging negative thinking

▶ behaving differently to change your feelings

▶ maintaining changes

▶ guidance for friends, family and carers to help support you.

Each chapter starts with a discussion and follows with exercises for you to practise, which will move you from what you have just learnt and take you from the theoretical into reality. In other words, the exercises help you to lift the ideas from the page directly into your own life.

CAN'T I JUST DO THE EXERCISES?

No. In order for the exercises to be meaningful and effective, you will need to read through the introductory text at the beginning of each chapter. This will provide a context and rationale for why you are doing the exercises and how they will work. Doing the exercises in isolation is unlikely to be helpful as they will not make sense without the additional information provided.

I'VE NEVER DONE CBT BEFORE – DO I NEED ANYTHING BEFORE I GET STARTED?

In order for this book to be helpful, you need to allow yourself plenty of time to read through and try the individual exercises. Also you need to be patient. CBT is not a 'quick fix' nor is it a 'magic cure'. It requires effort and input from you in order for progress to be made, but like most things in life, the more you put into it the more you will get out of it. If you allow yourself plenty of time and patience to complete this book you will see the benefits and be able to make positive changes.

WHAT CAN I EXPECT AT THE END?

After completing this book, you will be equipped with new ideas and strategies to help you overcome problems, and deal with negative and/or difficult situations that you are currently facing. However, the journey will not end there. The idea behind CBT is that it is not only effective while you are in therapy, but rather that you learn skills and techniques that you can use for life. This means that when you finish this book, you will only be at the beginning of your journey. You may notice significant changes throughout the book and you can continue to develop, change and achieve using the strategies this book teaches you for life.

Enjoy the journey – the new you starts here!

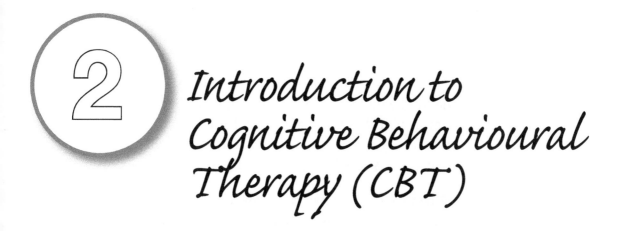

Introduction to Cognitive Behavioural Therapy (CBT)

In this chapter you will:
- *read a brief introduction into what Cognitive Behavioural Therapy (CBT) is.*
- *consider the types of disorders that CBT can help with.*
- *look at the focus and benefit of self-help CBT resources.*

You will learn:
- *more about the application of CBT to different problems and situations, and begin to consider how this applies to you.*

What will I have to do?
- *It is standard practice throughout CBT therapy for individuals to complete 'homework', e.g. work between sessions in order to build upon and develop the skills taught in each session. Throughout this workbook there will be various activities and worksheets to complete to help you to begin to practise your CBT skills. However, this chapter serves as an introduction to CBT and as such there is no homework set at the end of this chapter.*

→ So what is CBT?

There are a great many books and papers available which detail the development of CBT and its origins. The scope of this workbook doesn't allow for an in-depth review of the history of its development, so here we will give a brief overview as to what CBT actually *is*.

When we break down the term *cognitive behaviour therapy* we can see the main components of the therapy:

| Cognitive | Behavioural | Therapy |
| What we think | What we do | What we change |

The 'cognitive' part of CBT refers to our cognitions, or thoughts, and focuses on what we think in certain situations. CBT also focuses on our patterns of thinking and the way that our thoughts affect our mood and our behaviour.

The 'behavioural' part of CBT refers to our behaviours, or what we do, and again focuses on the way we behave in certain situations. CBT looks at the role that our behaviour plays in maintaining a particular problem or affecting our mood.

The 'therapy' part of CBT refers to changes that we make using a variety of techniques and strategies. The emphasis here is on the word 'change'. CBT is a very practical and experiential therapy, whereby you try new ways of doing or thinking and monitor the impact of these changes. CBT is a hands-on therapy that looks at a situation from a variety of different perspectives and puts into practice new methods. Many people want to get some help with a situation but struggle to see how things can be different and so the idea of change may be hard to imagine. This book will explain how these changes can be made, using a variety of strategies, and will give you an opportunity to try out these techniques in a way that is comfortable and do-able for you.

Previous therapies, such as Cognitive Therapy (Beck, 1976) and Behavioural Therapy (Wolpe, 1958) have looked at thoughts or behaviours in isolation. However, CBT practitioners believe that many different aspects, including our thoughts and behaviours, interact with, and impact on, each other in different ways in different situations. The section below describing the basic underpinnings of CBT explores this idea further.

→ The basic underpinnings of CBT

CBT does not just focus on one area but instead it looks at the interactions between many different components. The premise of CBT is that our thoughts, feelings, behaviours and physical symptoms, together with the situation within which they occur, all affect and interact with each other. This is demonstrated in the five-areas diagram below which is often referred to as the 'hot cross bun' model (Padesky and Mooney, 1990) due to its appearance and the four different segments. The fifth area is the situation, and is be defined by what or where it is that you want to change. For example, if you want to change how you think and behave in a meeting at work, then 'in a meeting at work' would be the situation that you would identify.

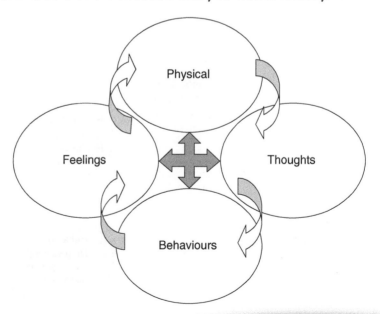

To give you an example of the way the different areas affect each other, a few examples have been drawn out below:

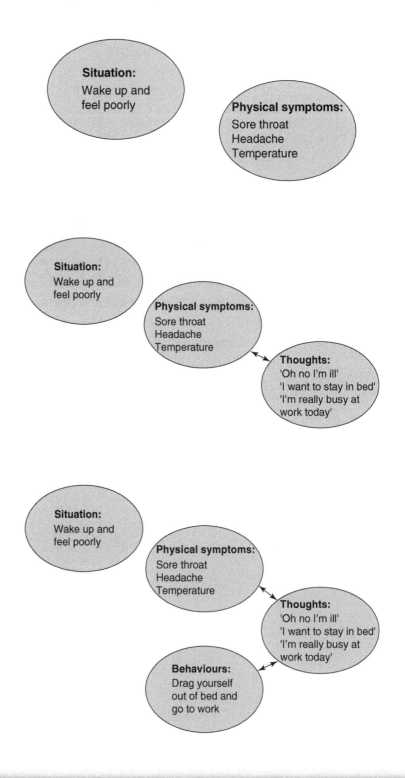

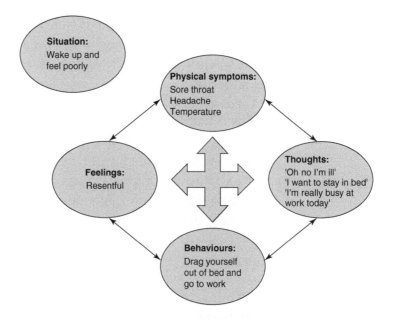

This example shows how physical symptoms can impact on our thoughts, feelings and behaviours. We can also see in the diagram below how thinking differently about something can change our behaviours and subsequently our feelings.

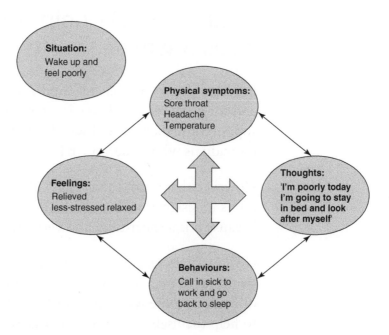

A basic principle of CBT is that because all these areas interact with each other, when we are able to change any one of these areas and we will see changes in all aspects of a situation.

This is helpful because people may find it much easier to access one area more than others. For example, we may be more aware of our physical symptoms than our thoughts, or more aware of how we feel rather than our behaviour in a particular situation. As one small shift can cause change in all these interlinked areas, then it is easy to see results and this helps us to build momentum to make other necessary changes.

If we believe in every situation that our thoughts, feelings, behaviours and physical symptoms all interact with each other and with the situation itself, then in order to see change we need to become aware of how we think, feel and act in a situation and then tackle one of these areas.

→ What can CBT help with and how does it work?

In recent years CBT has received a lot of positive press, and for good reason. There is a strong evidence base that supports the therapy and which shows impressive results for individuals who undergo CBT.

However, that is not to say that CBT can 'solve' all problems, nor is it designed to. Part of the reason CBT is so popular is because it is a short-term and very practical therapy.

CBT involves teaching individuals a number of different strategies to manage situations which they find challenging or difficult in some way. The aim of CBT is to help individuals to help themselves. In other words, the individual becomes equipped with the necessary skills and then becomes a kind of 'self-therapist'. This is beneficial for several reasons.

Firstly, by learning the skills and being able to put them into practice, individuals are able to increase their confidence in their ability to cope and deal with a variety of difficult or challenging situations. This also means that, once learnt, the individual has these skills for life, and is not dependent on a therapist, or being in therapy, forever.

Another benefit of CBT is that the principles are beneficial, regardless of whether you are trying to face a particular problem or situation, or whether you are just living your daily life. CBT techniques inspire confidence and courage, meaning individuals feel better in themselves, and notice an increase in their confidence and their self-esteem.

CBT has been shown to be effective in treating many different types of disorder ranging from eating disorders to psychosis. However, CBT has been proven to be most effective in the treatment of anxiety disorders, such as panic disorder, obsessive-compulsive disorder and agoraphobia, the treatment of more general worry and in the treatment of depression and low mood.

→ I don't think I have a specific problem – will this book still be useful?

Every individual will experience at least one episode of low mood or anxiety in their lifetime, and most of us will experience several, due to life events and the stresses and strains of daily living. Therefore it is good to learn and apply the CBT techniques to help reduce symptoms of anxiety, worry and low mood. CBT techniques can benefit everyone in some way, even if you don't feel there is a specific problem to address. CBT can be used to help build confidence, happiness, self-esteem and courage, which are all traits that could use a 'boost' from time-to-time. So even if there isn't a specific issue, do not worry – this book will still help you by teaching you helpful strategies you can apply to everyday life.

→ How can self-help CBT help and does it really work?

As mentioned above, CBT aims to teach individuals strategies and skills so that they can become their own 'therapist' for life and have portable skills which they can carry into many differing situations and problems. In this way self-help CBT can be extremely useful. You can learn and practise the skills being taught and see for yourself when they are helpful and work for you.

→ Do I need to see a therapist?

This book is in no way designed to be a replacement for one-to-one individual therapy. There are pros and cons of every therapy approach and, after reading this book, you may feel that you need extra support and would like to find a therapist. (If this is the case please see the list of charity contacts and support numbers at the back of the book.)

If you have been suffering with low mood for some time, it is common to feel a lack of motivation, and sometimes a one-to-one therapist can provide support and encouragement to help you complete the CBT exercises. If you don't like the idea of seeing a therapist or are unsure about what this would entail, then this book will give you a good head-start by introducing you to the basic elements of CBT and some of the key strategies that you would cover in one-to-one CBT therapy. Ultimately CBT is a very self-driven therapy, and self-help materials, such as this book, have been proven to be tremendously helpful (Williams, 2001).

However, if you feel very low/depressed, or feel that you need extra support in some way, then you should contact your GP and arrange an appointment to discuss therapy options. *Never postpone telling people how you are feeling.* It is far better, and far safer, to tell those around you and be open and honest with your GP about your feelings and what you are struggling with. Your GP will want to help you and will be able to directly refer you for extra support if this is what you feel you need.

Ultimately the decision is yours, but whether you opt for individual therapy, or choose a self-help route, this book will assist you by introducing you to CBT principles and teaching you valuable skills which you can apply in different situations.

→ I've heard CBT is too simple to be effective – does it really work?

There are lots of myths that surround CBT and the techniques involved and these can lead to some doubts about the effectiveness of CBT as a therapy. Below are some of the myths that surround CBT and answers to them. CBT *is* a very effective and popular therapy. If you are considering it, a good (CBT!) approach would be to 'try it and see' rather than make up your mind first (but more of that later!).

MYTH 1: CBT DOESN'T FOCUS ON THE CAUSE OF THE PROBLEM, IT ONLY FOCUSES ON THE SYMPTOMS

CBT as a therapy does not ignore the cause of the problem. The formulation process, which is when the therapist and individual map out what has led to the development of the problem, starts with looking at early experiences and 'critical incidents'. Critical incidents are the incidents or events that originally triggered the way we are feeling now, and in that sense CBT places a strong emphasis on the history, cause and development of a problem.

However, one of the most common phrases heard in therapy is, 'I don't know why I feel like this, I just do'. For this reason CBT does not get 'stuck' if there is no obvious history or cause available. Instead CBT is able to start work on what is causing the most difficulty (e.g. feeling anxious or depressed, being unable to leave the house), without needing to first focus on the history of the problem. In other words, CBT can treat the symptoms without needing to know the cause, although by no means is this cause ignored.

A colleague of mine describes this wonderfully using the following example:

Imagine you broke your leg and received a bump to the head. When you get to the hospital and they ask you what happened, you say 'I can't remember'. Wouldn't you want them to get on and treat your leg? Think how much pain you would be in and the damage you would do walking around on a broken leg whilst waiting to remember the reason why it's broken! In this way, CBT works by fixing the leg first and then addressing the issue of how it became broken in order to stop it happening again.

In this way CBT is different because it addresses the symptoms first, but it does not ignore the history or development of a problem.

MYTH 2: I'M NOT PARTICULARLY UNWELL OR BOTHERED BY ANYTHING – A BOOK ON CBT IS OF NO USE TO ME

As mentioned previously, one does not need to have a specific issue or problem to address. There may be a situation in which you would like to feel more confident or you may like to increase your self-esteem. Or indeed you may just be interested in finding out more about CBT therapy, which has received so much publicity lately. Whatever your reasons for being drawn to this book, it will give you an overview of the therapy and chance to learn and develop some CBT skills, which will be useful in a wide variety of situations.

MYTH 3: CBT IS JUST COMMON SENSE SURELY? I DON'T NEED ANY MORE OF THAT!

It is true that CBT is a logical and straightforward therapy, which is what makes it so accessible for so many people. However, when we are dealing with our thoughts and our emotions we are often unable to apply a 'common sense' approach. Imagine, for example, that you are scared of spiders. If you came across one in your bath tub do you think you would be able to think calmly and rationally in that moment? Probably not! CBT aims to give people strategies and techniques to apply a logical and balanced process to situations, which is very difficult to achieve on our own without some form of input or support. What may sound simple on paper can actually be very challenging to put into practice. After all, if it was that simple, we'd all be doing it.

Summary

The 'cognitive' part of CBT refers to our cognitions, or thoughts, and focuses on what we think in certain situations. CBT also focuses on our patterns of thinking and the way that our thoughts affect our mood and our behaviour.

The 'behavioural' part of CBT refers to our behaviours, or what we do, and again focuses on the way we behave in certain situations. CBT looks at the role that our behaviour plays in maintaining a particular problem or affecting our mood.

The 'therapy' part of CBT refers to changes that we make using a variety of techniques and strategies.

CBT is a hands-on therapy that looks at a situation from a variety of different perspectives and puts into practice new methods.

Our thoughts, feelings, behaviours and physical symptoms, together with the situations within which they occur, all affect and interact with each other.

Never wait to tell people how you are feeling. You need to tell those around you how you are feeling and be open and honest with your GP about your feelings and what you are struggling with.

What have I learnt?

→ Why doesn't CBT just look at your thoughts?

_____

_____

_____

_____

_____

_____

_____

→ What are the five areas that all link and interact with each other?

1 _____

2 _____

3 _____

4 _____

5 _____

→ How does CBT work?

_____

_____

_____

_____

_____

_____

_____

Where to next?

This chapter will have given you an outline of CBT and how and when it can be used. Some key points to remember from this chapter are:

▶ CBT can be applied in many different situations and to many different problems.

▶ CBT works by teaching you the skills and techniques that, once learnt, you can use forever.

▶ Although it is a logical approach it is a lot more than 'just common sense'.

The next chapter discusses how to get started on this process and looks at identifying common symptoms of anxiety and depression, and helps you to focus on your own situation.

How do I begin?

In this chapter you will:
- ▶ *explore the common symptoms of anxiety and depression and consider how to identify your own symptoms.*
- ▶ *focus on what might be the causes of anxiety and depression in your own life.*

You will learn:
- ▶ *about the symptoms of anxiety and depression and explore how to recognize your own symptoms.*
- ▶ *how to create your own model of a problem and how to reframe the way you think about a problem.*

What will I have to do?
- ▶ *You will need to work through the various worksheets and exercises given in this chapter and this will help you recognize your symptoms and understand how your thoughts, feelings, behaviours, physical symptoms and situations are all interacting with and affecting each other.*
- ▶ *Once you have completed these exercises, keep them somewhere safe as they will be useful to refer back to later.*

→ ## Do I have a problem?

The following sections look at common symptoms of different mental health problems that people may experience. The intention here is not to replace the opinion of a mental health practitioner, nor is it to provide a formal diagnosis. However, by becoming aware of symptoms and what they may indicate, this part of the book is designed to help you understand what you may be struggling with and help to explain why you are feeling the way you do.

Exercise 1

SYMPTOMS OF LOW MOOD

Symptoms	Tick
Feeling depressed or low for most of the day	
Loss of pleasure in activities/things you used to enjoy	
Significant weight loss or weight gain	
Disruption to sleep pattern – sleeping a lot more or less than usual	
Feeling fatigued or lacking in energy most days	
Feeling worthless or guilty for no obvious reason most of the time	
Difficulties with memory and concentration	
Difficulty 'getting going' in the morning – wanting to stay in bed	
Feeling overwhelmed	
No longer interested in appearance, e.g. not combing hair/ wearing make-up, etc.	
Reduced social interaction/not seeing other people as much as before	
Thoughts of suicide or being better off dead	

Adapted from DSM-IV criteria for depression (American Psychiatric Association, 1994)

To begin to understand any low mood you are experiencing, look at the checklist of symptoms above. Low mood or depression may encompass some or all of these symptoms. Place a tick next to the ones you feel you are experiencing.

....

SO AM I EXPERIENCING LOW MOOD?

If you have ticked five or more of the symptoms listed in Exercise 1, it is likely that you are suffering from an episode of depression or low mood. Episodes of depression and low mood range from mild to very severe, and it is likely that the more symptoms you have ticked, the more severe your depression will be.

If you ticked the last symptom and have been experiencing thoughts of suicide or being better off dead then you need to contact your GP immediately and seek support for this. It is not uncommon to think this way when depressed and it is important to seek help from your GP, who will be able to assist and refer you for relevant support and help.

SHOULD I KNOW WHY I AM DEPRESSED?

Sometimes a particular event, such as being made redundant or losing a loved one, can trigger an episode of low mood or depression. However, sometimes we can feel depressed and not really understand why or where it has come from. There are many factors that can influence our mood, from what we have eaten, to how many hours of sleep we are getting. If you have recognized and ticked more symptoms than you were expecting do not be alarmed. It is very common to experience an episode of depression and depression is a very treatable problem.

Exercise 2

SYMPTOMS OF WORRY

To identify whether you are experiencing anxiety, go through the checklist below and place a tick next to any symptoms that you recognize and are currently experiencing.

Symptoms	Tick
Finding yourself worrying excessively about things other people don't seem to worry about	
Finding it difficult to control the worry	
Unable to distract yourself away from the worry	
Feeling restless/keyed up/on edge most of the time	
Becoming easily fatigued	
Difficulties with memory and concentration – finding your mind will go blank	
Feeling irritable	
Muscle tension in your body – tension knots or aches	
Feeling sick	
Sleep disturbance – difficulty getting to sleep/waking early/ disrupted sleep.	
The worrying interferes with some aspects of your life, e.g. socializing/working	
Worry/symptoms cannot be explained by anything else, e.g. medication	

WHEN I'M ANXIOUS OR WORRIED I CAN FEEL QUITE PANICKY – AM I HAVING A PANIC ATTACK?

According to the American Psychiatric Association, (DSM-IV, American Psychiatric Association, 1994) a panic attack is described as:

A discrete period of intense fear or discomfort, in which four (or more) of the following symptoms develop abruptly and reach a peak within 10 minutes.

Exercise 3

Look at the list below and circle any symptoms that you have experienced. If you have circled four or more of symptoms above and you feel these 'attacks' are short-lived and are not otherwise explained by a medical problem (e.g. asthma), then it is likely that you have been experiencing panic attacks.

Palpitations/pounding heart/increased heart rate

feeling dizzy, unsteady, lightheaded, or faint

sweating

derealization or depersonalization

feeling of choking

fear of losing control or going crazy

chest pain or discomfort

fear of dying

trembling or shaking

numbing or tingling sensations

sensations of shortness of breath or smothering

chills or hot flushes

nausea or abdominal distress

Panic attacks are linked to anxiety and can occur for many reasons. However, do not be alarmed if you have been experiencing panic attacks. As with depression, anxiety is a treatable problem and, by making small changes, you can regain control and reduce the number of panic attacks you experience.

→ I seem to have symptoms of depression and anxiety – is that normal?

Depression and anxiety can go hand-in-hand and it is extremely common to experience symptoms of both. It can be difficult to overcome anxiety when feeling low in mood and demotivated, and equally feeling high levels of anxiety or worry can impact on mood and make us feel depressed. It can be helpful to consider which feels like the more pressing problem, or which one you would like to address first, and then focus on that one. However, if you are unsure how to progress and feel both depression and anxiety equally, then the recommendation is to focus on depression first, as the lift in mood will help you to feel more confident in overcoming your fears and worries.

→ I don't seem to have anything – can I still use this book?

Absolutely! If you don't recognize any of the symptoms listed in the exercises here, then think of a situation where you would like to feel happier or more confident, or perhaps an area in your life where you would like to feel more satisfied. You can work with this situation instead of focusing on a particular disorder using some of the key principles identified throughout this book. Try giving a name to whatever it is you identify as missing or being problematic, e.g. 'stress' or 'frustration', even if it isn't technically a diagnostic term, as this will help you to complete the worksheets in the next part of this chapter.

Exercise 4

Start to make your own model. Remember the five-areas model from before? This can be a really useful tool in helping you see how all these different areas interact with each other. Using the template below, think of a recent situation which made you feel particularly anxious, depressed, panicky or angry, etc. and plot out your own thoughts, feelings, behaviours and physical symptoms within that situation. Ask yourself: what was I thinking?; how was I feeling?; did I have any physical symptoms (e.g. tenseness or headache)?; what did I do in that situation? Then complete the five-areas model below:

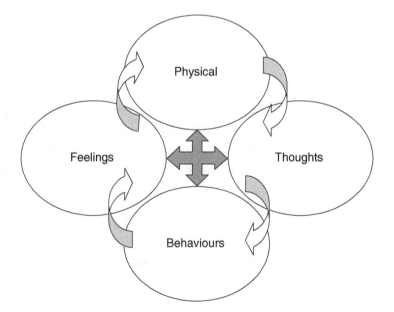

Try practising this a few times using different situations as examples so that you are able to start identifying the different aspects of situations.

NB: Not everyone is able to readily identify their thoughts, feelings, behaviours and symptoms. If you struggle to identify one of these areas then start with whichever feels strongest and work around the model from there. Remember there are no wrong answers. If you cannot identify them then do not worry; this book will teach you skills to help you identify these areas and this is always something you can come back to at a later point.

Now you know your problem you can try to change how you see it. One of the first steps in working with the problem you have identified is to externalize it; that is, to see it as separate from yourself. For example, if you are feeling anxious, then begin to see that anxiety as separate from you. Anxiety is a big, bullying chaotic mess that stands behind you and whispers 'what if?' questions and makes you question and doubt yourself.

Depression can make you feel as though there is a dark, heavy blanket covering you which keeps you down and makes it difficult to see beyond it.

Start to think of anxiety, depression, anger, stress or whatever you have identified as your main problem(s) as being these external beings that are separate from who you are. This is important because your problems do not define you and they are not a part of you – they are something that needs to be dealt with.

If you take the idea of anxiety as being a bully, for example, start recognizing all the times that anxiety is bullying you. Think of all the times it lowers your confidence, tells you you're not good enough and makes you doubt yourself. Start to recognize the thoughts you have and identify the problem that is causing them. Sometimes it can be helpful to draw out or have a mental image of what your anxiety, low mood, stress or anger looks like, and some people give it a name. This means that instead of thinking of yourself as being particularly anxious you can think to yourself 'wow my anxiety is really playing up today' or 'anger is really trying to spoil my day today', etc. Research shows that the externalizing of problems leads to greater recovery and higher self-esteem (Carey and Russell, 2002).

Exercise 5

Look at the table below and fill in some of the thoughts or beliefs you have about yourself, and then reframe them so that they belong to the problem causing them.

Thoughts/beliefs I notice...	Reframed thoughts/beliefs
e.g. When I did that presentation today everyone thought I was an idiot.	Anxiety is telling me that everyone thought I was an idiot when I did that presentation.

By externalizing your problem in this way, you are able to separate out the impact that the problem is having on you, and begin to see yourself as more than just your problem. Describing yourself to others in terms of your problem, e.g., 'I'm a very anxious person' will not help you overcome the issue, and may make it seem harder to change. However, once you realise you are *more* than your problem, you can begin to recognize all the skills and abilities you have which will allow you to overcome this problem once and for all.

Exercise 6

Complete the diary below over the next week and note down any thoughts or feelings that you have which upset you or are linked to a difficult situation. Practise reframing them so that you are able to start seeing the issue as external to yourself.

	Thoughts/feelings I noticed	Reframed thought/feeling
e.g.	I was really stupid at work today. I kept thinking I was an idiot.	Anxiety made me feel stupid at work today. Anxiety kept telling me that I was an idiot.
Monday		
Tuesday		

Wednesday		
Thursday		
Friday		
Saturday		
Sunday		

Summary

Sometimes depression can be caused by a particular event such as being made redundant or losing a loved one, and this can trigger an episode of low mood or depression. However sometimes we can feel depressed and not really understand why or where it has come from.

Depression and anxiety can go hand-in-hand and it is extremely common to experience symptoms of both.

If you feel you have more than one problem, then it can be helpful to consider which feels like the more pressing problem or which one you would like to address first, and focus on that one.

Try giving a name to whatever it is you identify as missing or being problematic, e.g. 'stress' or 'frustration', even if it isn't technically a diagnostic term, as this will help you to complete the worksheets and focus on your problem.

What have I learnt?

→ What is one of the first steps to overcoming any problem?

_____

_____

_____

_____

_____

_____

→ What name did you give to your problem/what problem did you identify to work on?

_____

_____

_____

_____

_____

_____

→ Once you recognise a problem, how do you externalise it?

_____

_____

_____

_____

_____

_____

_____

Where to next?

This chapter has focused on helping you to identify your main problem(s) and has shown you how all your thoughts, feelings, behaviours and physical symptoms interact with one another. The next chapter will focus on setting goals, both for the completion of this book, but also more long-term goals and show you how to set achievable goals.

Setting your goals

In this chapter you will:
► *look at the importance of setting goals.*
► *find out about the SMART goal-setting technique and understand how to set your own SMART goals.*

You will learn:
► *how to set SMART goals. This will be both relevant to the exercises in this book, but will also be a useful tool for the future.*

What will I have to do?
► *You will need to work through the various activities to complete the SMART goal table. This will help you set your goals for your 'therapy' and you can refer back to this as you work through the rest of the book.*

→ ## What is a goal?

When we talk about 'goals' we mean something that we want to attain or achieve in the future. This can be something in the near future (e.g. 'by the end of today I want to have completed this chapter'), or it can be more long-term (e.g. 'by the end of the year I want to have moved house'). Goals give us focus and something to aim for. When used properly, goals can be motivating and encouraging, and can help us to achieve whatever we want to achieve on a regular basis. Goals can also be used to bring about the change in our thoughts, feelings and behaviours that we are looking at throughout this book, and so it is important to get them right. This chapter is designed to help you set some goals that the CBT techniques will then help you achieve.

→ Working with goals

To some extent we work with goals every single day. We all have our own 'to do' lists, either carried round in our heads, scribbled on the back of an envelope or entered into a diary on our smartphone. These may not sound like goals, after all these are just the everyday things that we have to do, but they are. For example, on a typical to-do list we may have:

1 Get dinner ready.

2 Pick the kids up.

3 Phone Mum about sister's birthday.

Again, these may not sound like goals, but lists such as this are essentially things that we would like to achieve by the end of the day. The goals that we set and carry around with us can impact on our mood and our sense of achievement. Therefore it is important that the goals we hold for ourselves are meaningful and helpful, and that the goals we set for therapy are working towards a positive change or experience. So why are goals so powerful? How do they affect our mood?

Have you ever set yourself a New Year's resolution? It can be quite an exciting process. As you sit there making your list you begin to picture an exciting and different future, and often a different 'you' as well. This will be the year you stop smoking/lose weight/get a new job/stop drinking alcohol.

We can feel really motivated and encouraged at the thought of a better, brighter future. However, when at ten minutes past midnight we are standing there with a cigarette in one hand, and a glass of wine in the other, we can feel as though we have failed already – and we only started the resolutions ten minutes ago! This immediate impact on mood may not matter on New Year's Eve after a night of celebrations, but over time, if we feel we are continually 'failing' to meet our goals then this can leave us feeling as though *we* are the failures.

Feeling this way is very demotivating and can make us feel further away than ever from achieving what is important to us.

When people tell me they cannot achieve their goals, it is usually a given that there is something wrong with the goal that has been set and *not* with the person who is trying to achieve it. Setting goals is not as easy as just writing it down or making a mental note of something you would like to do. That gets us nowhere (as countless broken New Year's resolutions have shown us). Instead we need to focus on the right type of goal in order to make it achievable. There is no limit to what you can achieve; it just needs to be approached in the right way.

→ The difference between goals and a 'wish-list'

The main difference between a list of goals and a 'wish-list' tends to be how much control you have over achieving what's on the list. To try this out write the top five items on your wish-list below:

My wish-list:

e.g. Win the lottery

1 _____

_____

2 _____

_____

3 _____

_____

4 _____

_____

5 _____

_____

As you look at your wish list, ask yourself whether you have any control over these? If the answer if no, or very little, then these are likely to be wishes rather than goals. Everyone has a wish list to some extent, but we cannot rely on wish lists as we have no control over them. Goals on the other hand are a good way of getting results and the right goal helps to motivate us as well as achieve what we want.

→ Making goals SMART

When we set our goals they need to follow the SMART principle (Doran, 1981). The SMART principle breaks vague or broad goals down into specific, manageable tasks, by getting you to think about the goal under different headings. For example the goal 'lose weight' is a goal but it is not a SMART goal. This is because SMART goals need to be:

S   Specific

M   Measurable

A   Attainable

R   Realistic

T   Time-limited

To give you an example, let's turn the goal 'lose weight' into a SMART goal:

Looking at the examples below, think of some goals that you have previously set but haven't been able to achieve. Do they look like Goal 1 or Goal 2? The likelihood is that they look like Goal 1. We tend to only think about the 'end goal' or the desired effect rather than the specifics. However, it is only when our goals are broken down and made more specific, and follow SMART principles, that they move from being vague items on a wish list to specific and achievable goals.

It can be difficult to start thinking in terms of SMART goals, particularly if it is something that we are not used to doing. In order to start the process, try not to limit yourself – first think of what you want to achieve and we will turn these into SMART goals later.

Goal	Specific?	Measurable?	Attainable?	Realistic?	Time-limited?	SMART?
Goal 1: Lose weight	No. There are no details here to specify how much weight.	No. There are no details which say how this will be measured.	Unknown. There is no way of knowing whether this is attainable or not as it's too vague, and no plan is in place.	Who knows? This depends how much weight I want to lose and by when.	No time limit has been set and so this is not a time-limited goal.	X This is not a SMART goal.
Goal 2: I would like to lose 10lbs over the next six weeks. I will do this by cutting out chocolate and crisps and going to the gym three days a week.	Yes. The amount of weight is detailed and there is a clear plan in place as to how this can be achieved.	Yes. This will be measured in pounds and I will use the scales at the gym to measure the weight loss.	Yes. I have no health problems or anything standing in the way of me achieving this goal.	Yes. This is a realistic amount of weight to lose in six weeks.	Yes. There is a time limit in place of six weeks.	This is a SMART goal.

PHASE 1 OF GOAL-SETTING: DREAM BIG... AND THEN MAKE IT A REALITY

Setting goals is all about recognizing what is important to you and what you would like to achieve or change. You need to start from somewhere and so before setting your SMART goals, it is important to start thinking about what is important to you and what you would like to change.

Exercise 7

In order to start this process, use the table below to start categorizing your thoughts/desires/goals. At this stage do not worry if they seem unrealistic or if they have been something you have already tried and 'failed' at (remember: it was probably the goal not you!). Take some time to really think about what is important to you and the difference you would like to see in your life. Make these as big or as little as you like – these are your ideas and there are no right or wrong answers.

Defining your thoughts ready for goal-setting:

Things I like in my life and would like more of	Things I don't like in my life that I would like to change	Values that are important to me as a person	People I would like a different relationship with	Things I would like to change about myself	Where I would like to be in five years
e.g. I like spending time with my firends	e.g. I don't like feeling lonely	e.g. helping others	e.g. my brother – we don't talk as much as I would like	e.g. I'd like to stop worrying so much and keep relaxed and happy when I'm out	e.g. I'd like to be in a fabulous new job with lots of great colleagues and friends around me

Exercise 8

Looking at the table that you have just completed, you may already have identified some goals or areas in your life/home/mood that you would like to improve. Following on from the table, fill in column 1 of the following table to identify your initial goals. We will complete the table as we work through this chapter.

Table for setting my goals:

Initial goals:						
e.g. talk to my brother more						

PHASE 2: MAKING MY GOALS SMART

Looking at the SMART principles that we reviewed above, it is clear that the example given in the second table in Exercise 8 is not a SMART goal, and is much less likely to be achieved (see below).

Initial goals:	Specific?	Measurable?	Attainable?	Realistic?	Time-limited?	SMART?
e.g. talk to my brother more	No.	No.	No.	No.	No.	X This is not a SMART goal.

Exercise 9

Use the table below to work through your initial goals and turn them into SMART goals. The example given shows the process of turning the goal 'talk to my brother more' into a SMART goal. Try and complete this table for your own goals, turning your initial goals into SMART goals.

Making my goals SMART:

Initial goals:	Specific?	Measurable?	Attainable?	Realistic?	Time-limited?	SMART?
Talk to my brother on the phone once every fortnight for 15 minutes. I will call on my mobile every Thursday at 8 pm when the kids are in bed and I won't be disrupted.	Yes. There is a specific plan in place to make more contact with my brother.	Yes. I can measure the amount of times I phone my brother.	Yes. Initial problems e.g. being disrupted by the children have already been planned for.	Yes. This is a realistic goal and should be relatively easy to complete.	Yes. There is a time limit in place of every other Thursday.	This is a SMART goal.

Once you have completed the table in Exercise 9 you should have a list of SMART goals which you are able to start working towards right away. Some of the goals you have set may be to do with your mood and how you are feeling and you will be able to start working towards and completing those goals whilst working your way through this book. As everyone's goals are individual, this book is not geared towards specific goals. However, the strategies you will learn will focus on improving low mood or depression and reducing anxiety, as well as tackling other strong negative emotions. This in turn will leave you feeling more confident and with more energy to focus on yourself and your goals.

Summary

There is no limit to what you can achieve; it just needs to be approached in the right way.

It is only when our goals are broken down and made more specific, and follow SMART principles, that they move from being vague items on a wish list to specific and achievable goals.

If you have tried and failed to achieve a goal previously then there is most likely something wrong with the goal, and not with you. Go back to those goals and re-create them using the SMART techniques.

What have I learnt?

➜ What do the following letters stand for in relation to goal-setting?

S _____

M _____

A _____

R _____

T _____

➜ What is the difference between a goal and a wish list?

_____

_____

_____

_____

_____

_____

_____

→ Why is it important to set goals?

_____

_____

_____

_____

_____

_____

→ If I cannot achieve my goal, what may need to change?

_____

_____

_____

_____

_____

_____

Where to next?

The next chapter will focus on the common pitfalls and obstacles which get in the way of us achieving our goals, and will help you overcome these in order to make a list of goals which are not only achievable but will enable you to make the changes you want to make within your life.

Overcoming the hurdles to goal-setting: common mistakes and pitfalls

In this chapter you will:
- ► *learn how to avoid the most common pitfalls and mistakes that come with SMART goal-setting.*
- ► *understand what might get in the way of you starting your goal-setting and achieving our goals.*

You will learn:
- ► *about the possible obstacles that you might encounter, and barriers that could prevent you from setting and achieving your goals. This chapter will focus on how to overcome them.*

What will I have to do?
- ► *You will need to work through the various activities and complete the questionnaire, activity pie chart, tables and worksheets to help you recognize and overcome your own barriers to successful goal-setting.*

→ 'I just want to be happy!'

As we know from the work we've already done looking at SMART goals, having a goal such as 'I just want to be happy' is not likely to lead to achieving happiness. We need to know the specifics of such a goal and be able to turn it into a SMART goal. However it is not always easy to turn goals relating to our emotions into SMART goals, as it can be hard to see how to make the changes.

This is a really common pitfall and many people can struggle to deal with this at first. The best way to overcome this difficulty is to think of an initial goal and ask yourself lots of questions about it. So, for example, assume that being happier is your initial goal, and answer the questionnaire below. Alternatively, use the same sheet for different initial goals, by replacing the word 'happy' with the emotion/mood that is relevant to your initial goal.

Exercise 10

Questionnaire about my initial goal(s):

1 How will I know when I am [happy] (insert other goal here)?

_____

_____

_____

_____

2 What would be different if I was happy?

_____

_____

_____

_____

3 If other people were looking at me, what differences would they notice about me that would tell them I was happy?

_____

_____

_____

_____

4 What would I be able to do if I was happy, that I cannot do now?

_____

_____

_____

_____

5 How will I know when I have reached 'happiness'?

_____

_____

_____

_____

By answering these questions you will be able to identify some specific changes or elements that you would like to change or achieve. Once you have identified these, then go back to the table in the 'making goals SMART' section and start changing these into SMART goals which will make these achievable.

→ All work and no play...

One of the biggest pitfalls people make when writing their list of goals is that they don't include enough fun! You know the old saying, 'All work and no play makes Jack a dull boy'? Well it should say, 'All work and no play means goals never get achieved'. Often when people show me their 'to-do' list of goals they read like lists of gruelling tasks. For example, how inspiring would you find the list below?

1 Complete tax return.

2 Paint wardrobe.

3 Tidy sock drawer.

My guess is not very inspiring! We need to have a mix of activities that make up our list of goals. This will be discussed further later in this book, but in CBT we talk about activities falling into one of three categories:

1 **Pleasure**: an activity which is pleasurable/brings pleasure.

2 **Mastery**: an activity that makes us feel we've achieved something.

3 **Necessity**: routine tasks or activity which need to be completed or there would eventually be a negative consequence.

An example of a pleasurable activity could be socializing, a mastery activity could be learning a new skill and a necessary activity could be eating dinner. The reason we need a mix of these activities is that when we are busy or stressed it is often the pleasurable activities that go first, then the tasks that give us a sense of mastery, and so before we know it we are stuck in a cycle of necessary, but ultimately uninspiring and unrewarding, tasks. This is not great for our mood. By the same principle, having a mix of goals will bring different rewards, a sense of pleasure and satisfaction, and motivation to complete those tasks which are more routine and necessary.

Exercise 11

Think about your goals and divide up the pie chart below into the different categories. If your 'pleasurable' activity goals are less than a third of your pie chart, then you need to set some more pleasurable goals in place as this will help to improve your mood and motivate you. The example shows you what an 'unbalanced' pie chart would look like.

Example of a pie chart of activities when we are stressed, anxious or depressed:

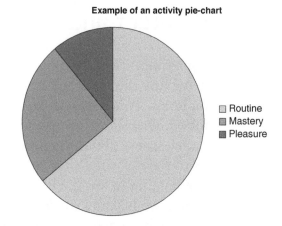

Example of an activity pie-chart

☐ Routine
☐ Mastery
■ Pleasure

Your activity pie-chart to complete:

NB: As well as having pleasurable activities built into your goals, be sure to recognize your achievements and reward yourself. Reaching any goal is an amazing thing to do and should be recognized, so reward yourself with something that gives you real pleasure. This can also act as an encouragement and good motivation for those days when you are tempted to avoid your goals – so don't forget to treat yourself!

→ 'I can't imagine my future being any different and so can't set any goals'

Sometimes it can be quite difficult to picture the future being any different and so it can feel challenging to decide on goals. This is particularly true when we experience low mood. One of the symptoms of depression is a feeling of hopelessness about the future. These thoughts can lead us to have a 'what's the point?' mentality, and it can be challenging to see the benefit of making changes. This means we become stuck in our current behaviours, and don't achieve what we want to or complete pleasurable goals and activities, and we become stuck in a vicious cycle:

'What is the point?'

No goals set

Nothing to work towards/nothing is achieved

Feeling hopeless about the future

If it is difficult to picture the future being different, then try and think of any time in the past when you felt different, perhaps a time when you were less stressed or felt happier overall. What was different then? What do you notice in yourself that's different between then and now? What would other people notice? Try and answer the questions laid out in the previous 'initial goals' questionnaire to help you start to think about the future differently. Remember your goals do not all have to be huge, life-changing goals. The sense of pleasure and mastery that we can get from achieving even the smallest of goals can have a big impact on our mood and make us feel more optimistic and hopeful about the future.

→ 'I have no money/time/energy'

Sometimes it can seem as though there are barriers in the way of us achieving our goals. Coming up against these barriers is very common in goal-setting and can often lead to individuals falling at the first hurdle and giving up – do not fall into that trap! If we as human beings stopped doing things because we had no money/energy/time then we would never get anything done.

Phrases such as 'I don't have time' are the grown-up equivalent of 'the dog ate my homework' (popular fitness quote, author unknown). These are not real excuses and should not get in the way of you achieving what you want to do. If time is a barrier, then devise a SMART goal to get some more time for you in your day. If money is an object then try and use SMART goals to help you overcome this. Equally, pretend you have all the money in the world and ask yourself what you would be doing differently and how you would be feeling. Often the thoughts and feelings are things we can achieve without the elusive lottery win. For example, if you think, 'If I had lots of money then I would see more of my friends and be a lot less stressed', then these are goals that can be worked towards without money – who needs cash when you have SMART goals?!

→ Setting goals that are too big – break them down into baby steps

Even when broken down into SMART goals, a common pitfall when it comes to setting successful goals is setting goals that are too large to be do-able. This doesn't mean that you have to aim low, far from it. However, if you are setting a goal that feels too large or too ambitious to complete straight away, then it is sensible to break it down into smaller much more manageable SMART goals. For example if you want to join a gym and lose weight then this can be turned into a SMART goal. However, this may still feel a bit too daunting and may put you off starting to work towards this goal. A better SMART goal to set originally may be to research gyms in your local area and find out membership costs. This can be changed into a SMART goal which is still working towards your ultimate goal but is a much more do-able first step.

By breaking down our SMART goals into smaller steps we are able to make progress and begin working towards our goal. These smaller steps can also help us overcome the obstacle of no time/money/energy, etc. The smaller and more do-able a goal is, the more likely we are to achieve and reach our ultimate goal.

→ Putting it off

A big part of goal-setting, and of CBT more generally, is that it needs to be the right time for you to make changes. If you find yourself continually wanting to do something but keep putting it off and never quite getting round to starting it, ask yourself what is getting in the way?

It can be useful to complete a list of pros and cons to achieving the goal, as this can help motivate you and also help you to see the benefits of completing the goal. The pro/con technique is also known in CBT as a cost-benefit analysis, where one looks at the costs of engaging with a particular task or goal and the benefits of completing this task/goal.

When we are putting something off, generally speaking, we are focusing on the negatives and all the reasons as to why we *can't* do it, rather than focusing on the positives. Again this is very common behaviour with low mood as we can get stuck in patterns of negative thinking.

Exercise 12

Complete the worksheet below to help you consider the pros and cons of your goals. If you struggle to complete this then it may be helpful to complete the worksheet with a friend, as they may be able to give you more objective reasons and help highlight the 'pros' of completing your goal.

Pros/cons worksheet:

My goal	Pros of completing this goal	Cons of completing this goal

→ Asking for the impossible

It is possible that there has been an event in your life that has led you to feel the way you do now, and it may feel impossible to change because you would need a situation to go back to the way it was which cannot be done. A common example of feeling like this can be after someone close to us has died. We may feel as though we would like to be happier, or achieve more, but this just doesn't feel possible without that person. This leads us to ask the impossible of ourselves and say 'I would be happy if he/she were still alive'.

This is a very normal reaction to sad events in our lives and we need to allow ourselves space to grieve and come to terms with the circumstances. It is important that we don't put unrealistic pressures on ourselves to 'get back to normal' before we are ready as this will not be helpful long-term and leaves us vulnerable to further dips in mood when we feel unable to achieve this. However, once we feel ready for some change to happen, we can then feel very stuck in a situation and unsure of how to go forward without that person in our lives.

In order to help with this, ask yourself what would be different if that person was still here? What would you notice about yourself and what you would be doing with them still in your life? As you start to think about these issues, ask yourself is there a way of achieving the value, even without the situation changing? For example, if you feel you would be happier or less lonely if that person was still alive, is there another way to feel happier or less lonely even without them?

This is not to say 'disregard your feelings and move on', as that is unrealistic and unhelpful. However, it is about not getting stuck in situations or feelings because of circumstances that we cannot change. It is important to stay focused on the *values* that are important to us. Again it may be helpful to speak to a friend, or someone close to you that you trust, about this issue and see if there are ways of making improvements to your mood and helping you to achieve your goals.

→ Relying on other people – no back-up plan

Some of our goals may include other people and this is good as it can help motivate us. However, we don't have control over what happens in other people's lives and so this can mean that what happens to others affects ourselves and what we are able to achieve.

A good example of this would be having a gym buddy that you go and workout with. If they telephone to say that they have to work late unexpectedly, this may mean that you don't go to the gym, and this may interfere with a goal you have around getting fitter or being more active, or maybe de-stressing after work.

An important element of a goal then is to have a back-up plan. So, for example, in the scenario above, a back-up plan would be to go to a class so that you still go to the gym and are motivated by other people, and are still on track to achieving your goal.

Exercise 13

A back-up plan is really important because other people may have any number of events that get in the way and if you are relying on them to help you this can become very frustrating and demotivating. So if you have a goal that includes someone else, fill in the Plan B scenario below – you may not need it but it's a good thing to have just in case.

Plan B Table:

Goal	Plan A	Plan B
e.g. Get fitter	Go to the gym at 7 pm with Sarah	If Sarah can't make it I will go to a step class at 7.15 pm instead to stay on track

→ 'Why didn't I start this sooner?'

As human beings we can be very critical and judgemental of ourselves. This means that when we start to achieve a goal we can be overtaken by thoughts of 'I should have started this sooner', 'Why didn't I just do this last week then it would be done already?', etc. We can also start comparing ourselves to other people and belittling what we are achieving. For example, we may think, 'OK, so I managed to go to the gym for half an hour, but Sarah goes everyday. I'll never be as good as her. I should be going everyday too'.

If you find this happening, then remember one of the key components of CBT work is that there is no judgement and no 'shoulds' because they are toxic and ultimately do us no good. So instead of criticizing yourself, recognize the achievement you are making and see how good it is to be making any progress and reward yourself.

Exercise 14

Complete the diary below to recognize your achievements, and remember: no criticism allowed.

Date	Today I achieved
e.g.	*I got up and went to work even though I felt really rubbish and just wanted to stay in bed for the whole day.*

Now that you are more aware of the common pitfalls and barriers that can get in the way of our goal-setting and achievements, you will be able to recognize when you are in danger of falling into these traps. Use the techniques outlined in this chapter to overcome these and move forward towards your goals.

Summary

One of the biggest pitfalls when people make their list of goals is that there isn't enough fun in there.

Having a mix of goals will bring different rewards, a sense of pleasure and satisfaction, and motivation to complete those tasks which are more routine and necessary.

Sometimes it can be quite difficult to picture the future being any different and so it can feel challenging to make some goals. This is particularly true when we experience low mood. If it is difficult to picture the future being different, then try and think of any time in the past when you felt different, perhaps a time when you were less stressed or felt happier overall. What was different then?

If you are setting a goal that feels too large or too ambitious to complete straight away, then it is sensible to break it down into smaller much more manageable SMART goals.

What have I learnt?

→ What are the three different types of activities that you should be including in your goals?

1 _____

2 _____

3 _____

→ If you are procrastinating and not getting started on your plans, what can help you overcome this?

_____

_____

_____

_____

_____

_____

_____

→ Why do you need a back-up plan?

_____

_____

_____

_____

_____

_____

_____

Where to next?

This chapter has highlighted some of the most common pitfalls of goal-setting and how to overcome them. Some of the key points from this chapter are:

1 Phrases such as 'I don't have time' are the grown-up equivalent of 'the dog ate my homework'.

2 By breaking down our SMART goals into 'baby steps' we are able to make progress and begin working towards our goal. These baby steps can also help us overcome the obstacle of no time/ money/energy, etc. If we make it more do-able we are far more likely to achieve and reach our ultimate goal.

3 Instead of criticizing yourself, recognize what you are achieving. Acknowledge how good it is to be making progress and reward yourself.

Now that you have some clear goals in place, the next chapter moves on to look at our thoughts and the unhelpful patterns of thinking we can fall into, and how to overcome these.

6 Why can't I stop thinking?

In this chapter you will:

▶ *begin to focus on your thoughts.*
▶ *understand why it is not possible to simply stop thinking, even though we would like to at times.*
▶ *learn to identify your thoughts and feelings in particular situations and will then look at some common thinking 'errors'.*

You will learn:

▶ *how to identify your own thoughts and feelings in particular situations, and you learn how to recognize your own thinking errors, and understand the impact these have on how you feel in certain situations.*

What will I have to do?

▶ *You will try a thinking exercise, complete a thoughts and feelings record worksheet and highlight particular thinking errors within your own recorded thoughts.*

→ Why can't I stop thinking?

Wouldn't it be great if our minds had an 'off switch'? You may have heard people use the phrase 'my head is spinning' or 'my mind is racing'. These phrases refer to the experience of an 'over-active' mind which can make us feel as though we have no control over our thoughts. This out-of-control feeling can be particularly strong when the thought is unpleasant or something which we really don't want to think about, yet can't seem to stop thinking about. So why is it that we can't just stop thinking?

YOUR MIND IS LIKE A TRAMPOLINE...

Imagine your mind as a room, and that the walls of your mind are made from the same stretchy bouncy material that trampolines are made from. Now imagine yourself in the centre of your mind surrounded by these stretchy walls. As a thought comes into your mind that upsets or distracts you, you want to get rid of that thought and try and push it out of your mind. Imagine taking that thought and pushing it away from you into the stretchy walls of your mind. What's the problem here? Well firstly you can't get rid of the thought, you can only push it away from you. Secondly, the harder you push a thought away from you, the harder it will bounce back and hit you, often when you least want it to. The same can be true of images. Not everyone thinks in words, some people also think in pictures and may get images of an event or a situation that they don't want to have in their minds and try to push these away, with the same result. Whatever we try and push out of our minds simply bounces back to us as though bouncing off a trampoline. This means we cannot gain control of our thoughts simply by ignoring them or pushing them away – it just doesn't work.

Exercise 15

I'm going to ask you to deliberately NOT think of a giraffe on roller skates. I'm going to ask you now to think of anything but a giraffe on pink rollerskates that is trying to stay upright but wobbling all over the place. Really try very hard not to think of a giraffe on pink roller skates. Close your eyes and try to keep your mind blank. Do not think of a giraffe on pink roller skates.

Be honest – did you think of the giraffe?

This happened because as soon as we try and push a thought or image out of our minds it bounces off the trampoline walls and pushes back into our minds. So in fact the harder we try NOT to think about something the more likely we are to think about it.

Alternatively, perhaps you were able to block out the image for a short time by distracting yourself or thinking of something else. However, what you may find is that when you stop distracting yourself, or your mind is 'quieter', then that image may pop into your head when you least expect it. The same happens with other thoughts and images: when we least expect it, they will pop into our minds.

→ But I can control my thoughts...

You may think that if you just try hard enough or distract yourself for long enough, or ignore your thoughts and refuse to listen to them, you can control thoughts. We all like to think that we have some control over our thoughts. This is particularly the case with anxious or depressed thoughts, or thoughts that evoke very strong feelings in us, and to some extent it is true. By deliberately thinking about something else or keeping ourselves distracted, it *is* possible to avoid thinking about a thought or image for a period of time. However, this is not sustainable. Sometimes we get so caught up in avoiding the thought, that we can engage in rituals, strategies or patterns of thinking or behaviour that can be very difficult to stop. This becomes a problem because it may no longer be the thought that is distracting or upsetting, but the idea that we cannot stop doing whatever our distracting mechanism may be.

Often, during an emotional time, people busy themselves and fill their day with lots of different tasks and activities. These may serve to keep them distracted from their thoughts. However, the difficulty then comes when people are no longer able to keep busy. This is when it is really difficult to cope as they may suddenly feel really overwhelmed with thoughts that they have worked hard to avoid. This is often why when we feel at our lowest or most tired we can feel overwhelmed with negative thoughts. This may not be because they have increased in number, but rather that we have run out of energy to keep holding them at bay. It's as though mentally our arms get tired from pushing all these thoughts back, and so when we finally let go they can all come rushing into our mind.

So can I ever control my thoughts?

The truth is that you can take back control over your thoughts. Sadly there is no way of guaranteeing that we will never have a sad or anxious thought ever again – life just doesn't work that way. What we can do though is take back control of our thoughts so that these thoughts do not take us by surprise or ruin situations for us. Have you ever been in a situation where you feel as though you *should* be feeling really happy but instead you have a stream of negative thoughts going through your mind? By using various strategies you can stop these thoughts from being overwhelming, leaving you free to enjoy the situation.

So how do I start?

The first step to taking control of your thoughts is to recognize your thoughts for what they are. That is that each thought is simply a mental act, in the same way that waving your hand is a physical act. Thoughts don't actually mean anything, they are just individual mental acts. The underlying premise of all cognitive therapy is that the act itself is not important, but rather our interpretation of that act is. So in the same way that a waving hand could be interpreted in several ways, such as saying hello or goodbye, or being dismissive or enthusiastic, etc., so too can our thoughts.

Often when we get 'stuck' in ways of thinking, there will be a series of thoughts that come through our mind and often there will be a pattern to these. For example, when we are stressed we may get the thought, 'I can't cope' running through our minds. If we accept this thought and consider it to be fact rather than a mental act then this can dramatically impact on our mood. As we know from earlier, our thoughts, feelings and behaviours all interact and impact on one another, so having the thought 'I can't cope' may lead to all sorts of emotions and behaviours that may not be helpful.

The first step in learning to take control of our thoughts is to be able to identify them. This is not as easy as it sounds – often it will be our feelings that we are aware of, not each individual thought, so it will take practise. One easy way of separating a thought from an emotion is that the thought should read like a statement. For example, the feeling may be 'stupid' and the thought statement may be 'I am stupid'. Or, to give another example, you may feel lonely in a situation and your thoughts in that situation may be, 'They don't like me'.

The first step to identifying your thoughts is to think of a recent situation which caused you to react with a strong emotion, either positive or negative. The reason we start with a stronger emotive situation is because it is easier to identify our thoughts, feelings and behaviours in situations that stand out for us, rather than in everyday situations.

Exercise 16

Fill in the table below to start identifying your thoughts and separating them from your feelings.

Identifying thoughts and feelings table:

Situation (Where was I? Who was I with? What was I doing?)	Feelings	Thoughts
e.g. Visiting relatives that live far away	Happy (to see them) Sad (that I don't see them more)	'It is so lovely to see everyone again' 'I wish we lived nearer' 'I hate not being closer to them'

As you can see from the example given in Exercise 16, it is not uncommon for people to experience conflicting emotions in the same situation, and it is very possible to feel positive emotions alongside more negative ones. A large part of the reason we feel this is that our thoughts will be having an impact on how we feel. Remembering the five-areas model (Padesky and Mooney, 1990) discussed earlier, you will know that our thoughts feelings and behaviours all interact with one another.

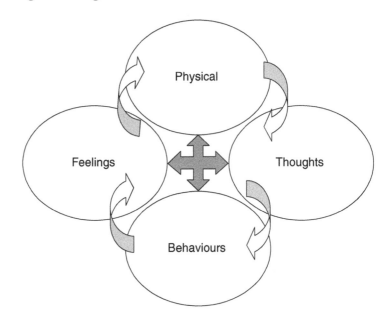

Now you have identified your thoughts and feelings in that situation, think about how you acted in that situation and how this then made you feel and any other thoughts you had following this. This is important as doing so allows us to tunnel a bit deeper into our experience and our thought process.

Exercise 17

Continue completing the table that you started in Exercise 16, but now fill in the extra columns.

Identifying thoughts and feelings table continued:

Situation (Where was I? Who was I with? What was I doing?)	Feelings	Thoughts	Behaviour (What did I do?)	Feelings	Thoughts
e.g. Visiting relatives that live far away	Happy (to see them) Sad (that I don't see them more)	'It is so lovely to see everyone again' 'I wish we lived nearer' 'I hate not being closer to them'	Went a bit quiet in front of everyone	Worried that I would become tearful	'I will ruin the situation for others' 'They will think I am making a fuss over nothing' 'They won't understand why I can't just be happy to be here'

From the table in Exercise 17 you can see how our thoughts can dramatically affect how we review and remember a situation, but also it can become clearer as to why we had certain thoughts in the first place.

Exercise 18

Spot the error! Listed below are some common 'thinking errors' which reflect patterns of thinking that we may fall into; these can cause and maintain low mood and anxiety. Look at the list below and then look at your identified thoughts in the table in Exercise 17. Highlight those thoughts which you feel fall into one of these thinking error categories.

Common thinking errors:

1 *Black and white thinking*: This is also known as 'all or nothing' thinking, whereby people tend to think in extremes. For example, a situation can either be brilliant or awful; people can either be lovely or horrible; we can think of ourselves as perfect or the worst person ever.

2 *Catastrophic thinking*: This is, as it sounds, thinking the worst or imagining a catastrophic outcome during seemingly everyday 'normal' experiences.

3 *Mind-reading*: Mind-reading refers to thoughts where we predict others' responses or thoughts. For example, 'I lost my footing walking by the road and everyone was looking at me and thinking I was an idiot'.

4 *Disqualifying the positive*: This refers to the way we can dismiss or belittle positive achievements or experiences and not recognize our own role in these. For example, 'I only passed my driving test because the examiner felt sorry for me', or 'I was lucky to get that promotion'. This kind of thinking usually only affects the positive meaning we take the blame for the negative events in our lives but dismiss the positive.

5 *Filtering*: This is when we see the world through a negative or anxious filter, e.g. we are unable to see the positive or good things that happen around us – our minds start to focus only on the negative events or news.

Summary

The feeling of an 'over-active' mind can make us feel as though we have no control over our thoughts. This out-of-control feeling can be particularly strong when the thought is unpleasant or something which we really don't want to think about, yet can't seem to stop thinking about.

Whatever we try and push out of our minds simply bounces back to us as though bouncing off a trampoline.

By deliberately thinking about something else or keeping ourselves distracted, it is possible to avoid thinking about a thought or image for a period of time. However this is not sustainable.

The first step to taking control of your thoughts is by recognising your thoughts for what they are. That is that each thought is simply a mental act, in the same way that waving your hand is a physical act. Thoughts don't actually mean anything, they are just individual mental acts.

Identify your thoughts by thinking of a recent situation that caused you a strong emotion, either positive or negative. The reason we start with a stronger emotive situation is because it is easier to identify our thoughts, feelings and behaviours in situations that stand out for us, rather than in everyday situations.

What have I learnt?

→ Why can't you just push thoughts out of your mind?

_____

_____

_____

_____

_____

_____

→ What is the problem with distraction? Why can't it work forever?

_____

_____

_____

_____

_____

_____

→What are some of the most common thinking errors?

_____

_____

_____

_____

_____

_____

→Which thinking errors did you identify as most relating
  to you?

_____

_____

_____

_____

_____

_____

Where to next?

Throughout this chapter you have begun the process of identifying your own thoughts and some of the thinking error patterns which your thoughts may follow. The next chapter will look at negative automatic thoughts (NATs) which form a key component of causing and maintaining low mood and anxiety. You will need to draw on your skills of identifying your thoughts, and over the next few chapters will learn how to challenge and overcome the negative thinking which is maintaining your current problem.

Negative Automatic Thoughts (NATs)

In this chapter you will:
- ▶ *focus on what negative automatic thoughts (NATs) are and where they come from.*
- ▶ *consider how to overcome NATs.*

You will learn:
- ▶ *how to identify your own NATs and understand where they come from.*
- ▶ *about strategies used to overcome NATs, which will be explored in more detail throughout the next few chapters.*

What will I have to do?
- ▶ *You will have to complete a thought monitoring sheet and continue to fill this in as the chapter progresses.*
- ▶ *You will have to complete a mini-formulation of the problem you are facing and how it developed.*

→ What do we mean by NATs?

Negative automatic thoughts are thoughts that pop into our minds and which are unhelpful or negative in content. As the name suggests, these are 'automatic', that is, that we don't have to deliberately call them to mind, instead they come into our minds unbidden.

The reason NATs are a problem is because they are negative and can help cause or maintain low mood or anxiety. We know from previous chapters that our thoughts affect all aspects of a situation including how we feel and what we do. Therefore if NATs, such as 'I can't cope' or 'I'm a failure', keep popping into our mind, they are going to continually have a negative impact on what we do and how we feel. As discussed in the goal-setting chapters, we know that negative thinking can also prevent us from achieving our goals and can leave us feeling demotivated. This means that if we continue to allow NATs to rule our thinking then we are likely to become 'stuck' in a situation where we feel too negative to change or achieve anything and may feel overwhelmed with negativity or anxiety.

For this reason it is important to identify, challenge and change our NATs so that we are able to move beyond our negativity and achieve what we want to, and reach our goals.

WHERE DO THEY COME FROM?

In order to understand where our NATs come from we need to think of them as a symptom of an underlying problem. This problem can be identified by 'formulating' how we feel and by looking at the history and development of a problem. This process is normally done collaboratively between a therapist and a patient, in order to help guide the patient to understand the development and source of their NATs.

Think of your thoughts as having layers, like an onion. NATs are the top layer and right at the centre are something called our 'core beliefs'. Much like an onion if you peel off the outer layers, the inner layers will be exposed and will gradually die off. Therefore by changing our NATs we are also going to be changing any negative core beliefs we hold.

Exercise 19

Here is a very simple technique to help you identify your core beliefs, and give you a greater understanding of where your NATs are coming from. Answer the questions below (example answers have been given to help you answer the questions):

What is the thought you identified? *e.g. 'I cannot cope with this'.*

→ _____

→ _____

→ _____

→ _____

Have you any evidence to support that thought? Are there any early/childhood experiences that support this? e.g. *'When I was younger I really struggled with my exams. My teachers told me I needed to try harder'.*

→ _____

→ _____

→ _____

→ _____

Do you behave in a certain way in order to try and avoid this thought from being true? e.g. '*I try and plan for every eventuality. I think of every possible outcome of a situation and try and plan for it so that I am prepared*'.

→ _____

→ _____

→ _____

→ _____

How does doing this make you feel? e.g. '*Sometimes I feel more prepared but I spend a lot of time worrying about things that never actually happen. I can never just relax and enjoy a situation. I feel as though I have to stay one step ahead*'.

→ _____

→ _____

→ _____

→ _____

What does this feeling tell you about you? What does thinking this say about you? What does this mean about your character? e.g. '*I can't cope without planning and even then situations feel stressful and out-of-control. I am scared to try new things and do not like change as I cannot control it or plan for the outcome. I cannot cope with anything. I'm useless*'.

→ _____

→ _____

→ _____

→ _____

The final question in Exercise 19 looks at the interpretation of your thoughts, e.g. what your thoughts and behaviours mean to you. It is your answer to this question that provides the most insight into your core beliefs. If you carry around a core belief that you are useless then it makes sense that you will experiences negative automatic thoughts telling you that you cannot cope or that you are not good enough. These NATs are the symptoms of the underlying core belief.

....

Our core beliefs are protected by the external layers of thoughts and so they are rarely challenged or tested – when we assume our NATs are correct, then we can take these as further 'evidence' that our core belief is correct. This is a self-maintaining cycle, as shown below, and the only way to break this cycle is to identify and challenge our NATs.

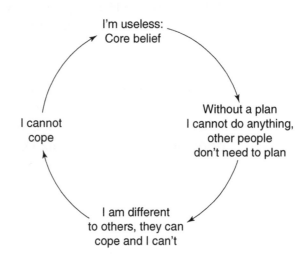

→ How do I spot my NATs?

You have already gained some skills in identifying your thoughts and some of the patterns that they fall into. The same skills are used when it comes to identifying negative automatic thoughts. We use a worksheet called a 'thought record' which acts as a thought monitoring tool and which we need to complete in as much detail as possible in order to allow us to challenge and change our thinking.

Exercise 20

To start with, use the thought record worksheet below and start by noting down this week any situations which caused you to feel negative/low/anxious, etc. and jot down the thoughts you noticed during or immediately after this situation. As you can see, this thought record has five columns. Complete the first three columns (Situation, NATs and Feeling) for a full week before continuing onto the next step (Exercise 20). A blank version of this thought record is available for you to copy and use in Appendix D.

Situation: Describe where you were/what you were doing.	Negative Automatic Thoughts (NATs): Write down any NATs that popped into your mind during this time. Rate out of 100 how much you believed this thought at the time, with 0 being not at all and 100 being completely.	Feeling: Note how you were feeling in that situation.	Alternative thoughts: Write down alternative thoughts that might be relevant in this situation. Rate out of 100 how much you believe this alternative thought, with 0 being not at all and 100 being completely.	How do you feel now?
e.g. sitting at my desk at work	'I cannot cope with this' (90/100) 'I cannot do this' (95/100) 'I am an idiot' (100/100)	Stressed and overwhelmed		

→ How do I change my NATs?

In order to change our NATs, and experience the resulting impact on our mood and our behaviour, we need to look for the evidence for such a thought, and consider alternatives to the initial negative thought. We do this to change the habit of just accepting our thoughts as facts and treating them as though they must be correct.

REVIEWING AND RE-EVALUATING YOUR THOUGHTS

Exercise 21

To start with you may find it easier to examine a situation and thoughts that are not your own. Look at the situation below and then write down all the possible explanations for the situation, i.e. all the possible reasons why this may have happened.

Situation: You are walking on the pavement and you see a colleague walking on the opposite side of the road coming towards you. As they get nearer you look across and smile at them. They look in your direction, but they do not smile back. Instead they seemingly ignore you and keep walking without acknowledging you in any way.

Write down a list of five possible thoughts you might have about this situation:

1 _____

_____

2 _____

_____

3 _____

_____

4 _____

_____

5 _____

_____

Did you find it hard to come up with five different thoughts? Sometimes it is tricky to see a situation in more than one way. A typical CBT technique is to ask yourself what a friend would think about that situation, or what someone else would think about that situation who didn't know either of you.

Now go back to your own thought record and begin to consider alternative thoughts about your situation and note those down. See the thought record below for an example, then complete the remaining two columns on your own thought record:

Situation: Describe where you were/what you were doing.	Negative Automatic Thoughts (NATs): Write down any NATs that popped into your mind during this time. Rate out of 100 how much you believed this thought at the time, with 0 being not at all and 100 being completely.	Feeling: Note down how you were feeling in that situation.	Alternative thoughts: Write down at least three alternative thoughts that might be relevant in this situation. Rate out of 100 how much you believe this alternative thought, with 0 being not at all and 100 being completely.	How do you feel now?
e.g. sitting at my desk at work	'I cannot cope with this' (90/100) 'I cannot do this' (95/100) 'I am an idiot' (100/100)	Stressed and overwhelmed. I felt stupid and depressed.	'It's not just me – everyone at work seems stressed' (90/100) 'Others are also struggling to cope' (100/100) 'Maybe there is a problem with the workload and not with me' (95/100) 'I am not an idiot' (100/100)	Less stressed. I know I'm not alone and that I am not an idiot. I feel more confident knowing that others are stressed as well. I feel proud for coping as well as I have given the pressures I've been under.

As you can see from the completed thought record in Exercise 21 the re-evaluated thought helps us to reconsider the situation and this changes how we think and feel in a situation. The aim here is not to try and be relentlessly positive, but rather to just be more realistic and balanced in your thinking. It is unlikely that everything will be wonderful but equally it is unlikely that a situation will be as negative or hopeless as your NATs are telling you it is. It is important to reconsider and evaluate our NATs and consider alternatives.

By training yourself to do this, the process of your thinking will change and you will be able to think about situations in a balanced and realistic way rather than falling into the trap of negative thinking. This is important as this will cause an improvement in your mood and your behaviour and will help to increase your confidence.

→ Dealing with our 'rules for living'

The previous section focused on the impact of our negative automatic thoughts and how to change them. We discussed NATs in terms of the outer layer of thought, and core beliefs as being right at the very centre of our thought 'onion'. Inbetween these two layers are our 'rules for living'. These rules for living stem from our assumptions about ourselves, others and the world. They are reinforced by our core beliefs and NATs, and they affect how we are and how we feel.

IF X THEN Y

Our assumptions often take the form of 'if' and 'then' statements. For example; 'If I fail then people won't respect me', or 'If I mess this up then people will not like me'. Much like our NATs, these assumptions can have a large impact on our mood and can maintain low mood and depression. Again, much like NATs, we can accept these assumptions and create rules for living without testing out whether or not the assumptions are true. This means that we may be thinking and acting in a way that is impacting on us without ever challenging these.

WHY IS THIS A PROBLEM?

Assumptions affect the way we see ourselves, those around us and the world. For example we may have a belief that the world is dangerous and can then create an assumption such as 'if I stay indoors, then I am safe', and then our rule for living may be to never leave the house alone. However, by living this way we will never find out whether the world really is a dangerous place, and may be living in fear for no reason. Therefore we need to challenge these assumptions and test our rules for living, much in the same way we challenge our NATs.

Exercise 22

Think about your own beliefs about the world, yourself and other people. Identify your own assumptions about the world and then your rules for living. Complete the table below (an example has been given to help you).

Belief about myself, others or the world	Assumption	Rule for living
e.g. Other people will reject me	If people get to know me then they will reject me	Never get close to people, be polite but don't make friendships

→ Looking for the evidence – using a Positive Data Log

Knowing that our assumptions and rules for living stem from our core beliefs leads us to challenge those beliefs. By using the thought record, you have already gained skills in creating more balanced and realistic thoughts. The same skills will be used here to challenge your beliefs.

Exercise 23

List below five beliefs that you hold about yourself, other people or the world:

1 _____

_____

2 _____

_____

3 _____

_____

4 _____

_____

5 _____

_____

Now use the table below to consider a more realistic belief (at this stage it doesn't matter whether or not you believe this more realistic belief) and write them down here – an example has been given to help you:

e.g. Old belief: Other people do not like me

New belief: Other people sometimes like me

Now write down your old belief and your new more balanced belief in the spaces below:

1 _____

_____

2 _____

_____

3 _____

_____

4 _____

_____

5 _____

_____

....

Now that you are aware of your old belief and have a new more balanced belief, you need to look for evidence that supports this new belief and weakens the old belief.

We use a Positive Data Log (Padesky, 1994) to monitor and record our new 'evidence' (see Exercise 24). Do not record evidence that supports your old belief – you already have enough evidence for that, as you can tell from your belief rating. Instead, focus on completing the Positive Data Log and recording evidence that supports your new belief. Then re-rate your beliefs at the bottom of the log. Do not expect an immediate or dramatic shift – you may have held this belief for many years without challenging it and so a complete change of view is unrealistic. Instead, look for evidence that supports your new belief and keep this and continue adding to it over the coming days/weeks/months. Continue to re-rate your beliefs as you go.

Exercise 24

Complete the Positive Data Log.

Positive Data Log
Old belief: e.g. **Other people do not like me**
Rate how strongly you believe this: _____%
New belief: e.g. **Other people sometimes like me**
Rate how strongly you believe this: _____%
Evidence that supports your new belief and disconfirms your old belief: e.g. **My colleague asked me to go for a drink with them the other day.**
Rate how strongly you believe your old belief: _____%
Rate how strongly you believe your new belief: _____%

Summary

Negative automatic thoughts are thoughts that pop into our minds and which are unhelpful or negative in content. As the name suggests, these are 'automatic', that is, we don't have to deliberately call them to mind and instead they come into our minds unbidden.

If NATs such as 'I can't cope' or 'I'm a failure' keep popping into our mind, they are going to continually have a negative impact on what we do and how we feel.

It is important to identify, challenge and change our NATs so that we are able to move beyond our negativity and achieve what we want to, and reach our goals.

In order to change our NATs and the resulting impact on our mood and our behaviour, we need to look for the evidence of such a thought, and consider alternatives to the initial negative thought.

What have I learnt?

→ What can you use to identify your NATs?

_____

_____

_____

_____

_____

_____

→ What are your assumptions?

_____

_____

_____

_____

_____

_____

→ What are your rules for living?

_____

_____

_____

_____

_____

_____

→ What can you use a positive data log for?

_____

_____

_____

_____

_____

_____

Where to next?

This chapter has shown you how to identify and re-evaluate your own NATs and helped you to formulate where they might be coming from. Sometimes when we are considering our alternative thoughts we simply don't know whether or not our NAT is true or false, and so one way to find evidence for or against that thought is to conduct a behavioural experiment. Behavioural experiments help us to challenge a thought and gain evidence for and against it in order to help re-evaluate it. The next chapter will talk you through how to conduct a behavioural experiment and help you to explore this further.

Behavioural experiments

In this chapter you will:
▶ *learn about behavioural experiments and how they work.*
▶ *learn to use behavioural experiments to help in your own situation.*

What will I have to do?
▶ *You will have to identify the key thoughts to be tested from a variety of example scenarios.*
▶ *You will have to identify your own thoughts to be tested.*
▶ *You will have to complete a behavioural experiment.*
▶ *You will have to design some future experiments to be completed as homework.*

→ ## What are behavioural experiments and why are they important?

The word 'experiment' may conjure up all sorts of unhelpful images of science class, Bunsen burners and small explosions – luckily none of these are features of behavioural experiments in CBT! Instead, as the name suggests, a behavioural experiment is an experiment which involves an aspect of behaviour. When conducting a behavioural experiment, we try out or test a behaviour and then carefully monitor the results.

Behavioural experiments are important because they provide an element of evidence which is otherwise unattainable. You may remember previously in the book we discussed the idea of 'evidence' for thoughts, and that in CBT you are not allowed to think or feel something without strong evidence for that thought. In some cases, when we try to find some evidence for and against the thought that is causing us so much anxiety, we simply do not know what the evidence is. This is usually due to avoidance or another unhelpful behaviour that has stopped us being able to gather any evidence against the belief.

CBT would say you are not allowed to worry about something unless you have a lot of evidence that you should be worried about it. Behavioural experiments allow us to test out any worries or beliefs that we may hold in a controlled and contained fashion, which makes completing the task or seeking the evidence a lot easier and less daunting.

WHY THEY WORK

A key component of a behavioural experiment is that it targets a specific thought or belief that you have. To help demonstrate this, let's look at the clinical example below:

Case study

John struggles with his confidence when it comes to maths and working out money. His girlfriend has booked a short weekend away for them both in France and John is feeling very anxious about paying in Euros. John feels that he will make lots of mistakes when paying and people will laugh at him and speak to him in French which he won't understand. John is now worrying about this so much that he is thinking of saying he won't go. He worries that if he tells his girlfriend about his worry, she will think he is an idiot. John has started to become irritable and grumpy around his girlfriend.

Poor John! What was meant to be a romantic treat from his girlfriend has turned into a real cause for anxiety. When John considered what his strongest worry about this situation was, he said: *'I worry about telling my girlfriend I'm anxious. She thinks I'm really strong and confident. I don't want her to think less of me or treat me differently.'*

John was engaging in a lot of thinking errors, such as 'mind-reading' and 'predicting the future' and so he needed to set up a behavioural experiment around talking to his girlfriend about his concerns. John believed that he would tell his girlfriend that he was worried and that she would laugh at him and tell him he's an idiot. John was 100% convinced that this was true and would definitely happen. However he had no evidence for this. So John developed a behavioural experiment where he would talk to his girlfriend and monitor the outcome.

When John spoke to his girlfriend, he was surprised to discover that his girlfriend told him she was also a bit worried about the money and suggested they both paid by card where possible to avoid any confusion about paying with Euros and accepting change. John's girlfriend also told him she was really pleased he'd told her as she'd noticed a change and was really concerned that something serious was wrong. John and his girlfriend enjoyed their weekend away anxiety-free, and John's rating of the belief went from 100% down to 0%.

This is how behavioural experiments work: they target a specific cognition and help an individual find enough evidence for or against that in order to reduce or increase their belief in a thought. Had John not completed this experiment he would have continued to carry around the belief that he couldn't talk to his girlfriend, which ultimately would have caused problems for them both.

Behavioural experiments can not only be used to disprove negative beliefs and thoughts but can also be used to gain evidence for positive beliefs as well.

→ How do I set up my behavioural experiment?

STEP 1: IDENTIFY THE 'KEY' COGNITION OR BELIEF TO BE TESTED

The first step in setting up a behavioural experiment is to identify the specific thought or belief that you are going to test.

Exercise 25

To develop this skill, try and identify some key specific thoughts or beliefs from the scenarios below. They need to be specific enough to be able to be tested in a behavioural experiment. When you have identified them, write them down in the space below the scenario.

SCENARIO 1

Kate has always been quite a shy person and finds it difficult to socialise when she doesn't know many people in a social situation. Kate recently changed her job and has been invited out to a work do and would like to go. However Kate is worried about this as she feels she is a dull person to talk to and that her new colleagues will either ignore her or walk away from her when she tries to talk to them. Kate is considering not going rather than face this anxiety.

Key cognition to be tested?

_____

_____

_____

_____

_____

SCENARIO 2

Andy borrowed his Dad's car and someone drove into it in a car park and drove off without leaving a note. Andy came back to find the car not badly damaged, but with a huge scratch down the side which will need repairing. Andy is worried about telling his Dad, as he thinks his Dad will yell at him and will not let him borrow the car again. Andy is avoiding driving home and ignoring calls from his Dad.

Key cognition to be tested?

_____

_____

_____

_____

_____

SCENARIO 3

Aoife has been wanting to go back to the gym since having her first baby eight months ago. Aoife used to be very active but had a difficult pregnancy and has not been to the gym in over a year. She has lost touch with her friends there and has no one to go with her. Aoife is worried people will judge her as she has put on weight and will laugh at her when she uses the gym equipment/joins a class. This fear has put Aoife off from going to the gym for the last four months and is leading to her becoming low in mood and demotivated.

Key cognition to be tested?

_____

_____

_____

_____

_____

How did you get on? Test your answers with the answers given below:

Kate's scenario: the thought to be tested is: 'new colleagues will either ignore her or walk away from her when she tries to talk to them'.

Andy's scenario: the thought to be tested is: 'he thinks his Dad will yell at him and will not let him borrow the car again'.

Aoife's scenario: the thought to be tested is: 'people will judge her as she has put on weight and will laugh at her when she uses the gym equipment/joins a class'.

Exercise 26

Now that you have developed this skill for others, think about your own situations and identify your own key thoughts or beliefs to be tested. Write them out below:

_____

_____

_____

_____

_____

_____

STEP 2: RATE THE BELIEF (0–100%)

Once you have identified the thought that you need to test out, then you need to rate how strongly you believe that thought out of 100%. So, if you only half-believe that your thought is true, then you rate it as 50% belief. If you don't believe it at all, then the rating is 0%. If you really strongly and absolutely believe the thought, and think that is definitely what will happen, then you rate it as 100%.

STEP 3: PLAN THE EXPERIMENT

Now that you have identified the exact thought or belief to be tested, and you have rated that thought, you need to plan a way of testing this out. If we take the first scenario, Kate's situation, then a behavioural experiment for her would be speaking to her new colleagues for ten minutes and seeing whether they will ignore her or walk away from her.

Exercise 27

Think about your own thoughts and situations and write down a behavioural experiment which would allow you to test out the thought and gather evidence for and against it. Write out the experiment below:

_____

_____

_____

_____

_____

_____

Points to remember:

▶ Your experiment needs to be long enough to provide a fair test. It would be no use Kate going and speaking to her colleagues for 30 seconds as this would not be long enough to test out the idea that they think she is dull and will ignore or walk away from her. It needs to be a realistic timeframe to provide an accurate test of the thought.

▶ The experiment needs to be do-able and realistic. There is no point setting yourself a behavioural experiment so challenging that you are unable to complete it. A quick way to test this is ask yourself how likely on a scale of 1–10 are you to complete this? If the answer is anything less than 7 then it is unlikely that you will go ahead and so you need to adjust the timing or the situation enough to make it more comfortable. BUT...

▶ ...don't make it *too* easy. If you are testing something out and it doesn't feel challenging or difficult in any way then it is unlikely that you are testing something significant or 'key' to your difficulty. That's not to say behavioural experiments should be unpleasant but the whole point is that they challenge a belief that you hold quite strongly that is maintaining some unhelpful thought or behaviour. If the experiment feels really easy then it is unlikely that this is the case. Go back and review it and ask yourself if you are really focusing on the main or key issue.

I KNOW THE PROBLEM BUT CANNOT THINK OF A WAY TO TEST IT

This is a common stumbling block as behavioural experiments are not something that we are used to doing in day-to-day life. To give you some ideas there are a few suggestions below:

▶ Ask other people. A really common experiment in CBT is to conduct a survey, whether this is a formal brief questionnaire, or whether this is informally asking those around you. For example, if people believe they hold an unusual belief or are the only person that worries about something, then CBT would say you're not 'allowed' to think that until you have asked other people. This is a particularly good approach for those 'mind-reading' worries we can hold, e.g. 'my colleagues will notice my hands shaking during the presentation and think less of me'. CBT would say, do the presentation and then find out by asking your colleagues if they noticed your hands shaking. Again you are not 'allowed' to have this thought or worry without testing it out first.

▶ Get some help. As well as asking people as part of an experiment, you can ask other people how they think you could test something out and see if those close to you have some good ideas. Remember though, it has to be significant and meaningful to you and your specific thought, otherwise it will hold little value.

▶ Ask yourself if you are avoiding. Often we can think of the exact way to test something but it feels too scary and so we can avoid it. If you think this might be the case for you, then go back to the experiment and break it down into smaller more do-able steps and see if you are able to work through those instead.

STEP 4: MONITOR YOUR BEHAVIOURAL EXPERIMENT

This section introduces you to your behavioural experiment worksheet. The worksheet is used to monitor and log your behavioural experiment either during or immediately after the event. It is important to keep a record of your experiments as it can be hard to remember the details and we want to be able to use this as evidence in the future.

The worksheet below shows the key headings and some instructions to follow in order to complete each column.

A behavioural experiment worksheet:

Date and situation	Key thought being tested: What do you think will happen?	Experiment: What did you do?	What did happen?	How do you feel now?	Re-rated key thought
Write down in detail here when and where you were, who you were with, etc.	*Write down your key cognition/belief that is going to be tested here. Rate how strongly you believe this thought/belief at the time (%).*	*Write down here what you did to test out the cognition/ test out the belief.*	*Write down here what happened during the experiment.*	*Write here how you feel now and anything that you weren't expecting or that surprised you.*	*Re-evaluate that initial key thought/ belief and re-rate how strongly you believe that thought/ belief now (%).*

Experiment 27

Complete a behavioural experiment and fill in the worksheet like the one given here (blank copies can be found in Appendix E). Note down any difficulties or problems you encountered and think about how you can overcome these in future experiments. The example worksheet below has been completed to provide guidance.

AN EXAMPLE WORKSHEET COMPLETED FOR KATE'S SITUATION

So, let's remind ourselves of Kate's situation:

Kate has always been quite a shy person and finds it difficult to socialize when she doesn't know many people in a social situation. Kate recently changed her job and has been invited out to a work do and would like to go. However Kate is worried about this as she feels she is a dull person to talk to and that new colleagues will either ignore her or walk away from her when she tries to talk to them. Kate is considering not going rather than face this anxiety.

Kate's behavioural experiment worksheet:

Date and situation	Key thought being tested: What do you think will happen? How strongly do you believe this? (%)	Experiment: What did you do?	What did happen?	How do you feel now?	Re-rated key thought
3 April: work do at local pub.	I will try and talk to my new colleagues but they will either ignore me or walk away from me because they will think I am dull (100%).	I will go to the work do for one hour and will aim to talk to at least three different people in that time. After one hour I will say I am meeting friends and excuse myself if I want to leave.	I met another colleague who was new to the firm within five minutes of arriving and we talked easily for over half an hour. She introduced me to a couple of other people. I ended up staying at the party for 3.5 hours and have arranged to meet up with some colleagues for a drink next week.	People found me interesting and I had a lot in common with other people who were also new to the company. I noticed other people seemed a bit apprehensive and a bit nervous too so I wasn't on my own. People can't have found me dull or they wouldn't have agreed to meet up with me again, or they would have made some excuse.	I now know that colleagues won't walk away from me or ignore me. I don't think they think I am dull. I would now rate my original belief as untrue (0%).

→ Keeping a record of your success

As well as completing the behavioural experiment worksheets and keeping those as evidence, try and complete the brief diary sheet below of your successes in completing these experiments. This will boost your confidence and belief in yourself that you are able to try new things and face challenging situations. This means next time you have a fear or worry about your ability to do something, you can glance at your record of success and know that you are capable of anything.

Exercise 28

Complete the 'record of success' diary below as you continue to complete behavioural experiments. Remember to reward your successes.

Record of success diary:

Date and situation	What I did	How I feel now
e.g. Work drinks with colleagues	Made myself socialize with new work colleagues, even though I was worried about this	Confident and interesting to others.

→ Reviewing your behavioural experiments

It often takes more than one behavioural experiment to challenge a key cognition. This is because our anxieties and low mood are great at putting down our successes and so we need to keep testing out our thoughts and our beliefs until we are satisfied that they wrong, or until they stop causing us negative emotions. The key is to take the next challenge. Once you have done something successfully, ask yourself if there is another way to test this that may challenge you further or take you one step nearer to your goal. The most confident people are those that take small risks. By living in our comfort zones all the time we never find out what we are truly capable of, so go on! Push yourself and take the challenge!

→ When can I stop experimenting?

You will be the best judge as to whether you can stop testing out a belief. If you feel a sense of avoidance then I would keep testing until you are able to truly face the challenge you have set yourself. However, it may be the case that some thoughts need repeated testing at different times and so you may find that throughout life there are times when it is useful to take the challenge and test out a belief or a specific thought and this is fine – you now have the ability and the skills to use this whenever you want, and to overcome any fear or belief, or thought that is holding you back.

→ What if it goes wrong?

There is no such thing as a behavioural experiment going 'wrong'. Every experience teaches us something valuable and gives us something to reflect on and consider for the future.

Exercise 29

Pick two NATs from the thought record you completed earlier, and plan a behavioural experiment around them which will help you to gain evidence for or against your thought. Complete the experiment by filling in the behavioural experiment worksheet (blank copies in Appendix E). Then review your original thought/belief.

Once reviewed, complete the seven-column thought record sheet outlined below and in Appendix F. The example from Chapter 5 has been followed through here to demonstrate this further.

Seven-column thought record

Situation (describe where you were/ what you were doing)	Negative Automatic Thoughts (NATs) (write down any negative automatic thoughts that popped into your mind during this time) Rate out of 100 how much you believed this thought at the time, with 0 being not at all and 100 being completely.	Feeling (note down how you were feeling in that situation)	Evidence to support your negative thought	Alternative thoughts (write down at least 3 alternative thoughts that might be relevant in this situation) Rate out of 100 how much you believe this alternative thought, with 0 being not at all and 100 being completely.	Evidence to support your alternative thought	How do you feel now?
e.g. sitting at my desk at work.	'I cannot cope with this' (90/100). 'I cannot do this' (95/100). 'I am an idiot' (100/100).	Stressed and overwhelmed. I felt stupid and depressed.	Feeling overwhelmed. I cried at my desk.	'It's not just me- everyone at work seems stressed' (90/100). 'Others are also struggling to cope' (100/100). 'Maybe there is a problem with the workload and not with me' (95/100). 'I am not an idiot' (100/100).	Colleagues have told me how stressed they are too. My boss would tell me if I was failing to cope with something.	I know I'm not alone and that I am not an idiot. I feel more confident knowing that others are stressed as well. I feel proud for coping as well as I have given the pressures I've been under.

Summary

When conducting a behavioural experiment, we try out or test a behaviour and then carefully monitor the results of this behaviour.

CBT would say you are not allowed to worry about something unless you have a lot of evidence that you should be worried about it. Behavioural experiments allow us to test out any worries or beliefs that we may hold in a controlled and contained fashion, which makes completing the task or seeking the evidence a lot easier and less daunting.

A key component of a behavioural experiment is that they target a specific thought or belief that you have.

Behavioural experiments work by targeting a specific cognition and help an individual find enough evidence for or against that in order to reduce or increase their belief in a thought.

The experiment should not be too hard or too easy: it needs to be do-able and realistic. There is no point setting yourself a behavioural experiment so challenging that you are unable to complete it. A quick way to test this is ask yourself how likely on a scale of 1 to 10 are you to complete this? If the answer is anything less than 7 then it is unlikely that you will go ahead and so you need to adjust the timing or the situation enough to make it more comfortable. Equally, if the experiment feels too easy then adjust it so that you get a sense of reward and achievement from facing a challenging situation.

What have I learnt?

➜ What are the four steps to a behavioural experiment?

1 _____

2 _____

3 _____

4 _____

➜ Why is it important to keep a record of your experiments?

_____

_____

_____

_____

_____

_____

_____

→ What can you do if a behavioural experiment feels unmanageable?

_____

_____

_____

_____

_____

_____

→ When can you stop experimenting?

_____

_____

_____

_____

_____

_____

Where to next?

This chapter has taught you the basics behind behavioural experiments, why they are useful and how to set one up on your own. The key points to remember are:

▶ You are not allowed to just 'have' a worry or a belief in CBT – you need to be able to prove it.

▶ Behavioural experiments are a useful way of testing out thoughts and beliefs and should be used to gather 'evidence' for and against the belief or thought.

▶ If a behavioural experiement feels too hard then break it down into baby steps.

The next chapter focuses on other behavioural strategies you can use to improve your mood and increase your sense of well-being. The focus here is less on challenging your thoughts and more on directly changing your behaviour to influence the other areas involved such as thoughts, feelings and physical symptoms.

9 Doing something different to change how you feel

In this chapter you will:
- ▶ *learn to shift your focus from your thoughts to looking at your behaviours and feelings.*
- ▶ *examine some typical 'unhelpful' cycles of behaviour to see if you can identify any particular trends or patterns which may be keeping you trapped in a particular cycle of thought or mood.*
- ▶ *learn how your own behaviour influences your mood.*
- ▶ *learn how changing this behaviour not only changes your mood but also causes changes in your thoughts and feelings.*

What will I have to do?
- ▶ *Try the exercises and shorter, practical ideas to give you an 'instant lift' in your mood and record what you notice using the worksheets provided.*

→ Why focus on your behaviour?

We know from the CBT model that our behaviour interacts with and affects how we feel and what we think, and can cause some strong physical symptoms. For example, if we do something really brave then we may feel proud of ourselves, our thoughts may be positive, for example, 'Wow! I can't believe I did that!' and we may feel physically different, perhaps from an endorphin or adrenaline rush.

Equally, negative behaviour can impact on us as well. For example, if you avoid doing something because it is scary, then physically you may experience some dread and tension leading up to the event, your thoughts may change and become more negative. For example you may think 'I am a coward' or 'I am weak', and then you may feel very disappointed and your confidence in yourself may be shaken. So as you can see our behaviour plays a vital role in what we think and feel and so it is important to focus on your behaviour and what you are *doing* as well as the other elements.

IF THE FOCUS IS ON MY BEHAVIOUR, DOES THAT MEAN IT'S MY FAULT?

Not at all. As we have said, nothing happens in isolation, and there will be many thoughts, feelings and situations that impact on us and cause us to behave in a certain way. However, by focusing on and potentially changing some of our behaviour we also know that this can positively affect our thoughts and feelings. Sometimes it is by changing what we do that we see the biggest changes in the way we feel. This is because some behaviours can be reinforcing of some negative beliefs and thoughts and so can be unhelpful long term and lead to us maintaining feelings of low mood and anxiety.

→ Examine your behaviours

Like most things in CBT, when we are thinking about our behaviours, we're looking for evidence, as the way we think we behave in certain situations may not be the way we actually do behave. Our behaviours may be interpreted quite differently by other people from the way we interpret our behaviours ourselves.

Exercise 30

To start with, complete the following scenarios by finishing the sentences with your behaviour. These scenarios will ask you to think of the last time you felt a certain way or were in a certain situation and then ask you to complete the sentence with your behaviour.

For example:

Last time I was hungry I... made myself a sandwich

Following on from the example above, complete the scenario questions below by filling in how you behaved in this situation. If this is not a situation you have been in, or you are unsure, spend a few moments thinking how you might act in that situation. Try and be as honest as possible. Remember this isn't how you think you 'should' act in a situation, this is about writing done how you have acted or would act in different situations.

Complete the sentences below:

1 The last time I was upset with someone I...

_____

_____

2 The last time I was angry with someone I...

_____

_____

3 The last time I felt afraid I...

_____

_____

4 The last time I felt embarrassed I...

_____

_____

5 The last time I felt stressed I...

_____

_____

6 The last time I was in physical pain I...

_____

_____

7 The last time I was poorly I...

_____

_____

8 The last time I felt something was unfair I...

_____

_____

9 The last time I felt anxious I...

_____

_____

10 The last time I felt miserable I...

_____

_____

→ Reviewing your behaviours

Now that you have completed Exercise 30, go through the scenarios again and see if you can identify any particular patterns or repeated behaviours. Often we have a go-to 'stance' which is a way of behaving or coping in situations that we have become used to and is now the way we automatically react.

Exercise 31

Now look at the list of behaviours below and circle the ones that feel most relevant to you/the ones you have identified from your behaviour review above:

Avoidance   Ignoring   Defensive   Anger

Ask someone else to do it instead   Running away

Comfort behaviour (e.g. eating or drinking)

Using something or someone to help me

....

The behaviours listed in Exercise 31 are all unhelpful in the long term. This is because each of them plays a role in maintaining low mood or anxiety. Below are suggestions of how to change your behaviour and what you can do instead.

→ Avoidance

Ignoring or running away from a situation, or asking someone else to do it instead, all come under the category of avoidance.

The problem with avoidance is that we never learn that we are capable of doing something or challenging ourselves. The benefits of taking a challenge or tackling a situation that we would normally avoid are that we change the way we think about ourselves. Instead of thinking 'I can't do this' or 'I can't cope', we think 'I *know* I can do this'. This is because we have acquired some evidence for ourselves and proven to ourselves that we *can* do something. Even if a situation is daunting and feels unmanageable we can always break it down and tackle some element of it. By doing so our thoughts will change, which will impact on our feelings and make you feel more positive, in control and elated from your successes. All of these positive emotions will contribute towards a greater degree of confidence and will give your self-esteem a boost. Remember it is your anxiety or low mood that is telling you that you cannot do something – it is not a fact until you prove it.

HOW DO I CHANGE MY BEHAVIOUR?

Next time you are in a situation that you want to avoid or are tempted to ask someone else to do instead, ask yourself what the situation involves and can you break it down in any way. Also ask yourself why you want to avoid and notice the role your anxiety or low mood is playing. Next challenge yourself, similarly to a behavioural experiment, and monitor the difference in how you feel.

Exercise 32

Use the table below to monitor the outcomes of situations that you would normally avoid:

Situation I would normally avoid	Why am I avoiding it?	Is this me or is this my anxiety/ low mood/ problem telling me I should avoid this?	How will I feel if I manage this?	What happened in the situation when I didn't avoid it?	How do I feel now?
e.g. Asking my boss for a pay rise.	I'm scared of what he'll say and that he'll be too busy and cross with me for disturbing him.	This is my anxiety. I never like talking about money and I am a bit scared of my boss.	I will feel proud of myself and will treat myself to new shoes.	I emailed my boss instead of asking him directly. I had a reply asking to meet him and had a pay review.	Proud of myself and unsure what I was worried about before. I know now I can do this and would do it again.

As you can see from your table in Exercise 32, this uses a technique similar to a behavioural experiment. The basic premise of CBT would say that if you are worried about doing something or are avoiding something and it's impacting on you, then do it and see if you should be worried. There is no point in worrying about something until you know that you cannot do it, and you only know that by giving it a try.

It often only takes a short burst of courage to try something new or tackle a situation and by stepping out of our comfort zone we instantly build our confidence.

Exercise 33

Pick a situation or something that you have been avoiding and *get it done this week*. Use the chart in Exercise 32 to monitor your progress and remember, when you think you cannot do this, it is your anxiety or low mood telling you this, it is not a fact. The more you challenge your feelings in this way the more confident and the less anxious you will feel.

→ Acting 'as if'

Exercise 34

If you find yourself asking someone else to do something for you, stop and ask yourself what the difference is between yourself and that person. Once you have identified the key differences between you and that person jot them down below, e.g. *'They are braver than me, they are not scared to ask for what they want'.*

_____

_____

_____

_____

Now think of a situation that you would normally ask this person to help you with/do instead of you. What would they do differently to you? How would they act differently? What would you notice about them? Again, use the space below to jot down these ideas, e.g. *'They walk confidently into a room, and they make eye contact with other people and come straight to the point. They never apologize for taking up other people's time'.*

_____

_____

_____

_____

Now think of the situation you would normally avoid by getting this person to help you. Now I want you to act 'as if' you are that person. Think about what you would do if you were the same as that person, and how you would act in the situation. *Now go and try it.*

We call this technique acting 'as if', because you simply act 'as if' you were the other person. By changing our behaviour and acting as if we were someone different, we find that our thoughts and feelings are different. This change in behaviour is just one way in which you will notice what you are doing having a positive impact on your feelings and thoughts. Equally, when we act 'as if' we notice that others around us treat us 'as if'. For example, if we act as though we are more confident and capable than we feel, then people around us will treat us as though we are confident and capable. If we act as though we deserve other people's time and respect, then we will be treated as such. So it is not only *your* behaviour you are changing here but also the behaviour of others around you.

Exercise 35

Face a situation you would normally get someone else to face and act 'as if' you were someone else. Make a note of your experiences below:

_____

_____

_____

_____

→ Change what you do in order to change how you feel

Remember in goal-setting when we talked about the importance of getting a balance between routine, mastery and pleasurable activities? Well it is important to get that balance in day-to-day life as well. When we are low in mood or feel particularly stressed or anxious, then we are far more likely to drop our pleasurable activities. If you've had a long tiring day at work then you are less likely to meet up with friends or want to go out. This is fine on the odd occasion, but with low mood, this gradually becomes the norm until all we are doing are the routine activities that we have to. Think of this as doing the bare minimum activity wise. Behaving in this way has serious consequences for our mood and we need to redress the balance of our behaviour.

Exercise 36

Think about how you are spending your time this week and complete the activity pie chart below, dividing your time between routine, mastery and pleasurable activities:

Your activity pie-chart to complete:

If there is less than a third of pleasurable activities then you need to schedule in more pleasurable activity.

··

→ Activity scheduling

Activity scheduling is a technique used to increase the amount of activity we do. As mentioned previously, it is common for us to reduce our activity when we feel low or anxious, but ultimately this has a detrimental impact on our well-being. We stop doing the activities we enjoy and so it is harder to feel positive about the future as we see no pleasure in it.

Activity scheduling is a simple method, using a straightforward diary to schedule in some activity which will help increase your mood.

Exercise 37

To start the activity scheduling process, complete the diary below by filling in your current activities – try and be as detailed as you can. A template for the diary can be found in Appendix G.

	Monday	Tuesday	Wednesday	Thursday	Friday	Saturday	Sunday
7.00–8.00 AM							
8.00–9.00							
9.00–10.00							
10.00–11.00							
11.00–12.00							
12.00–1.00 PM							
1.00–2.00							
2.00–3.00							
3.00–4.00							
4.00–5.00							
5.00–6.00							
6.00–7.00							
7.00–8.00							
8.00–9.00							
9.00–10.00							
10.00–11.00							

When you have completed a full week's diary, rate the level of pleasure and mastery of each activity out of 100%. Review the activity and consider are you doing as many mastery and pleasurable tasks as you were before or as you would like to be doing? Are your activities high in mastery and pleasure? If the answer is no then the aim of activity scheduling is to work towards your pre-depression/pre-anxiety levels of activity.

....

Increasing your activity in this way serves three main purposes:

1 You do more, leaving you less time to worry/be alone with negative thoughts.

2 You achieve more, meaning you gain active reward from tasks which leads to increased motivation and an improvement in mood.

3 You protect the time to do the tasks that are important to you, rather than just doing whichever task crops up next regardless of the impact on your mood.

Exercise 38

Complete an activity diary for the coming week (use the template in Appendix G). In addition to your usual tasks, add in at least two pleasurable activities, and plan for how you are going to complete them. Then put it into practice. Continue to do this adding in one or two tasks every week and ensuring that you complete them. By changing your behaviour in this way, you will regain control of your week, and begin to achieve what you want to during the week, which will result in an improvement in mood and well-being.

....

→ Reframe your 'symptoms'

Often our bodies give us the signals which tell us how we are feeling. For example, when we feel nervous, we may notice we need the toilet more, or our hands may shake. Similarly to interpreting our thoughts, the way we interpret our physical symptoms impacts on the way we feel.

Many emotions such as anxiety, anger or excitement, cause our bodies to release adrenaline. This adrenaline, although helpful in the short term, can lead to us feeling 'on-edge' and jittery and this can lead us to have unhelpful thoughts or act in unhelpful ways.

We can challenge our physical symptoms by 'reframing' them. This is a technique which allows us to change how we are feeling. For example, excitement and nerves will often cause the same physical symptoms in our body. The next time you are nervous, stand in the mirror and tell yourself that you are excited. Even this small behaviour changes the way we interpret our symptoms and helps us to feel differently about an approaching situation.

If you combine this with a change in thoughts as well, then this technique can help you face otherwise difficult situations.

For example, imagine you are about to go into a meeting you feel nervous about. You may notice your palms are sweating and that you need the toilet more frequently.

Your thoughts may be quite nervous as well: 'I hope I don't mess this up'; 'What are they going to say to me?'; 'Am I in trouble?', etc. Imagine now that you look in the mirror and reframe your symptoms. Say aloud to yourself, 'I am excited and these symptoms are symptoms of excitement'. Your body now interprets these symptoms differently and you will find your thoughts will shift as well, perhaps to: 'This is an exciting opportunity. I am excited to find out what is going on. I cannot wait to meet these people and hear their news.'

Exercise 39

Next time you experience physical symptoms relating to a situation, try reframing those symptoms as something else and notice any changes in your thoughts.

Summary

Our behaviours may be interpreted quite differently by other people from the way we interpret them ourselves.

Often we have a go-to 'stance' which is a way of behaving or coping in situations that we have become used to, and is now the way we automatically react.

Many emotions such as anxiety, anger or excitement cause our bodies to release adrenaline, which can leave us feeling 'on-edge' and jittery and lead us to have unhelpful thoughts or act in unhelpful ways. We can challenge our physical symptoms by 're-framing' them, a technique that allows us to change how we interpret our physical symptoms.

What have I learnt?

→ How do you act 'as if'?

_____

_____

_____

_____

_____

_____

_____

→ What is activity scheduling?

_____

_____

_____

_____

_____

_____

_____

→ What three types of activity should be included in activity scheduling?

_____

_____

_____

_____

_____

→ How can you re-frame feelings of nervousness?

_____

_____

_____

_____

_____

_____

Where to next?

This chapter has focused on a few behavioural techniques for you to try which will consequently impact on your thoughts, feelings and physical symptoms. Continue to practise these techniques over the next few weeks and keep a record of all your attempts at these behaviours and the resulting change in mood or thoughts.

So far we have looked at ways of changing our thoughts, feelings and behaviours through a variety of techniques. The next chapter will focus on factors that cause you to maintain unhelpful behaviours and help you to overcome some of the issues which may be keeping you 'stuck' in a role which you no longer want to be in.

10 Maintaining unhelpful behaviours – and how to break the cycle

In this chapter you will:
- ▶ *learn to focus on what causes you to maintain problematic behaviours.*
- ▶ *learn to identify behaviour which may be keeping you 'stuck' in a certain role or pattern, and which may be stopping you from making progress.*
- ▶ *learn how to recognize where you may have become 'fixed' in a role or pattern of behaviour, and how to address this.*

What will I have to do?
- ▶ *You will have to consider and draw out your own maintenance cycles and the behaviours that maintain them.*
- ▶ *You will have to draw out new cycles which incorporate a new behaviour which will help you overcome this difficulty.*

→ Thinking about a behaviour and what keeps a problem going

We have already learnt that our behaviour impacts on our moods and feelings, but sometimes it is difficult to see how what we do *maintains* a problem and makes it difficult to change. The sections below examine three different types of unhelpful maintaining behaviours. Consider these behaviours and also consider any others which may be maintaining a problem for you. Look at the maintenance cycles demonstrated and practise drawing your own so that you can see the role of the behaviour or thought that is maintaining a problem, then focus on changing it and monitoring the change within these cycles.

→ Behaviour 1: getting angry

WHAT DOES MY ANGRY BEHAVIOUR LOOK LIKE?

There are many different ways that people express their anger. Angry behaviour may involve:

▶ shouting

▶ slamming doors/cupboards

▶ being threatening towards someone else (either physically or verbally)

▶ ignoring someone else

▶ smashing something

▶ driving dangerously

Exercise 40

Look at the list above and circle which of these behaviours sound familiar to you, and which you may engage in yourself. Use the space below to write out any other behaviours you may engage in when you are angry:

_____

_____

_____

_____

_____

_____

_____

Often angry behaviour involves other people as we can get angry towards other people, or they may 'get in our way' when we're angry. As you can see from some of the behaviours listed above, there is a high chance that someone could get caught up in your angry behaviour and often the behaviour is threatening or damaging, either to others or to ourselves.

WHY DO I GET ANGRY?

There are lots of different reasons why people can become angry and why they behave in an angry way towards someone else. Often people blame their temper and say

'I have a short fuse' or similar, but often the development of anger is more complicated than this.

Anger can become a good way of defending ourselves when we feel vulnerable or unsure of ourselves. If we look at nature, often animals who are afraid of being attacked in some way will develop aggressive strategies which allow them to attack first (think of a scorpion attacking a potential predator with its stinging tail).

People who are afraid of being emotionally 'attacked' in some way react similarly. We may not have stinging tails but we may find ourselves being defensive or attacking and hostile towards other people, before they have a chance to attack us.

Another type of common angry behaviour is a feeling of being let down and feeling hurt and angry that our needs haven't been met by other people. This is particularly common in people with anxiety, but can affect everyone. Ever had that feeling when a partner or colleague has let you down and you think, 'Why don't they *know* that I'm not ok? They should know me well enough by now to know what I need from them'? The problem with this kind of anger is that it can lead to unhelpful 'mind reading', whereby we think that because this person hasn't met our needs then it says something about their feelings for us. This can affect our mood and how we feel about that particular relationship, yet we are not basing these ideas on facts, merely on our own untested beliefs.

WHAT'S GOOD ABOUT GETTING ANGRY?

In certain situations, anger is a very normal and understandable reaction to an event or situation which has occurred, and anger can sometimes pass or dissolve without causing any problems.

WHAT'S BAD ABOUT GETTING ANGRY?

Physically anger is not good for us in the long term. Often in situations when we are angry we may notice some strong physical reactions.

Exercise 41

Look at the list below and circle any symptoms you recognize:

heart pounding   red face   shaking

muscle tension   headache

sensitivity to sound and noise

feeling sick/upset stomach   sweating

lack of concentration   memory difficulty

A lot of the symptoms listed in Exercise 41 are related to high adrenaline levels. Whilst a small burst of adrenaline can be useful for humans to help us react quickly in situations, long burst of adrenaline can leave us physically exhausted and drained.

HOW DOES ANGER MAINTAIN MY LOW MOOD/DEPRESSION?

Where anger becomes a problem is when it is not limited to understandable situations and does not pass. If you find yourself holding onto resentment and anger towards someone else, this can dramatically impact on your mood.

Squashing down anger and never telling other people when they have hurt or upset us can lead to depression. Also if we never learn to deal with anger then we may start to avoid situations or people that we feel may make us angry or behave in an angry way.

There is a wonderful Buddhist quote which discusses how anger affects us:

'Holding on to anger is like grasping a hot coal with the intent of throwing it at someone else; you are the one getting burned.'

It is important to recognize the impact that anger is having on us and to try and work with different ways of approaching situations. Being angry and hostile towards other people means we never let people close to us. This can feel positive because we may feel by keeping people at a distance we will never get hurt. However, this will simply maintain the belief we have about other people being able to hurt us.

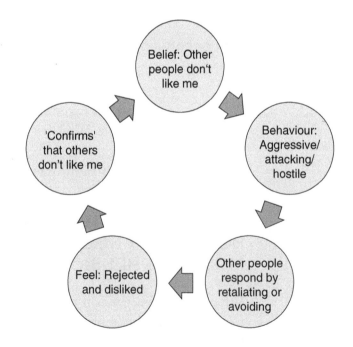

As you can see, if we never test this belief then this will impact on the type of relationships that we allow ourselves.

This behaviour may also prevent us from getting close to people we would like to have closer relationships with.

HOW DO I BEHAVE DIFFERENTLY?

The identified problem above is the angry or hostile behaviour, therefore this is the element we would like to change. Consider the implications of acting differently – how could we act differently in this situation? Look at the example below:

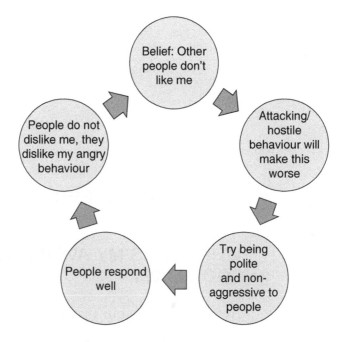

Exercise 42

Now consider your own anger. What can you do or how can you think differently in order to change this behaviour and the overall outcome? Draw out your new cycle (see below) and try putting this into practice. Monitor your successes and complete the cycle to review the outcome.

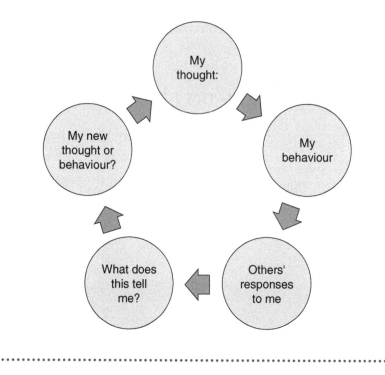

→ Behaviour 2: avoidance

WHAT DOES MY AVOIDANCE BEHAVIOUR LOOK LIKE?

Avoidance behaviour may involve the following:

▶ not answering the phone

▶ not socializing

▶ not doing things you want to do

▶ not pushing yourself or challenging yourself, e.g. not putting yourself forward for a promotion at work

▶ avoiding conflicts or arguments

▶ not telling people how you feel

▶ not confronting situations

▶ not thinking about/talking about certain issues or events

Exercise 43

Look at the list above and circle which of these behaviours sound familiar to you, and which you may engage in yourself. Use the space below to write out any other behaviours you may engage in when you are avoiding something.

_____

_____

_____

_____

_____

_____

_____

_____

. . . .

WHY DO I AVOID?

We start to avoid situations when we feel uncomfortable about them or unable to cope with them in some way. Often with low mood we can avoid situations because we simply don't have the motivation or feel capable of the effort involved. This is often what can lead us to have reduced socialization when we feel low – it is simply a case of not feeling able to go and so we avoid the situation.

Sometimes we may unconsciously avoid something and not realise that we are distracting ourselves from thinking or doing something that we don't want to focus on. (Have you ever noticed how when you want to avoid making a difficult phone call suddenly tackling the ironing basket becomes more pressing?!)

We also avoid situations that may make us feel intimidated or that we are not sure how to behave in.

WHAT'S GOOD ABOUT AVOIDANCE?

At first glance, avoidance can seem really positive. After all if something makes you feel intimidated or you don't want to do something then by avoiding it you don't have to confront or face that experience, and the negative emotions that come with it.

WHAT'S BAD ABOUT AVOIDING?

As we already know, avoidance is a classic safety behaviour which actually maintains low mood and anxiety. This is because by avoiding people or situations, we never get an opportunity to disconfirm the beliefs we hold about that situation or person. Continually avoiding means that we never gather any evidence for or against that belief and so we continue to hold on to an unhelpful belief which is marinating our low mood or anxiety. In CBT you're not allowed to just hold a belief without evidence, as this is tremendously unhelpful, so in fact avoidance is the best friend of anxiety and depression. As long as you keep avoiding, you're never challenging anxiety and depression and never proving them wrong.

The maintenance cycle of avoidance looks as follows:

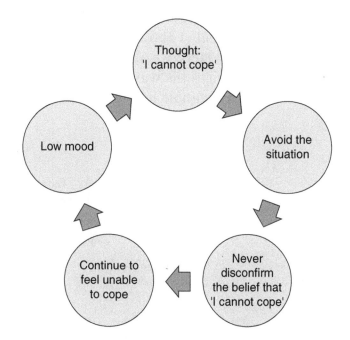

Every time you avoid something you are adding a little bit of strength to the idea that your anxiety or depression is right. Because of this, the longer you avoid, the harder it can feel to then face a difficult or challenging situation, as depression and/or anxiety will have been strengthened a lot before you challenge this.

NB: This does not mean that once a situation is avoided that it is impossible to go back and challenge, far from it. However it needs to be recognised that the longer we avoid a situation, the more unhelpful this can be for individuals.

HOW DO I BEHAVE DIFFERENTLY?

The key to changing our avoidant behaviour is to face whatever it is we are avoiding. We know that unhelpful thoughts can prevent us from facing situations, even when we have no evidence for them. However, as the above maintenance cycle shows, this only maintains our belief and keeps the problem going. By stopping avoidance we allow ourselves to act differently which changes the way we think and feel about a situation. See the example below:

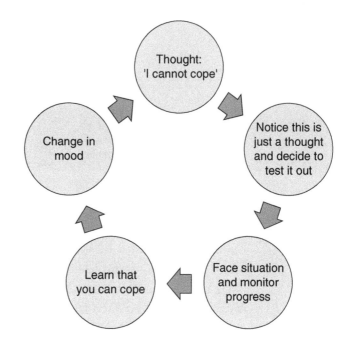

Experiment 44

Think of a situation that you are currently avoiding, or that you typically avoid. Notice the thoughts that you have related to this and draw out your maintenance cycle, paying attention to the role avoidance plays in maintaining your belief. Then challenge the belief and monitor the impact in your own cycle, which you can draw out in the space below:

→ Behaviour 3: being a superhero (and not saying no – even when you want to)

I call this behaviour being a superhero because that is often what this behaviour can feel like. You know the type – you may well even be a superhero! You are everyone's go-to guy.

WHAT DOES SUPERHERO BEHAVIOUR LOOK LIKE?

If someone has a problem or a situation they are dealing with then you are the person they call. You have a to-do list as long as your arm, but you are happy to drop everything to rush to a friend's rescue. You keep track of things at work, organize the birthday and leaving dos and remember all the details that other people do not. Sometimes it feels as though you have to do everything, but you know if it wasn't for you doing everything then nothing would ever get done. Superhero behaviour might look like this:

▶ saying yes whenever someone needs help

▶ being the person who 'rescues' others or situations and averts disaster

▶ being the most organized and the one in charge of everything in the household/at work/socially

▶ putting other people's needs first

▶ doing things that you don't necessarily want to do in order to keep other people happy

Exercise 44

Look at the list above and circle which of these behaviours sound familiar to you, and which you may engage in yourself. Use the space below to write out any other behaviours you may engage in when you are busy being a superhero/finding it difficult to say no.

_____

_____

_____

_____

_____

_____

_____

_____

Still not sure of your superhero status? Try the following exercise too.

Exercise 45

Before continuing with this section, look at some of the statements below and place a tick next to any which are familiar to you and that you agree with:

Without me nothing would ever get done ☐

Other people are useless ☐

I am the only person that could do what I do; my wife/husband/partner/friend/colleague would only get it wrong ☐

It is quicker and easier if I just do it myself ☐

Other people cannot be trusted to do things properly ☐

I have high standards ☐

I am a bit of a perfectionist and like to make sure things are done properly ☐

I put other people's needs first ☐

Other people rely on me ☐

I find it hard to say no to people ☐

I like helping people ☐

It is nice to feel needed/wanted ☐

If I didn't do everything I do people would think less of me ☐

I don't like other people to think I cannot cope ☐

I don't mind going the extra mile if it means getting something finished or helping someone ☐

If you have ticked more than one box then grab your cape – you *are* a superhero!

WHY AM I A SUPERHERO?

This often isn't a role that people ask for or put themselves forward for. Quite often people who become the superhero in their group are the people who are the most thoughtful and caring as well as the most organized.

WHAT'S GOOD ABOUT BEING A SUPERHERO?

What *isn't* good about being a superhero?! You feel an amazing sense of achievement knowing you are the person everyone else relies upon and without you it feels as though no-one would cope. There are many aspects about being a superhero which are highly valued, both by you and by those around you, such as wanting to help others, being a kind and thoughtful person, who puts other people first. These all seem like positive character traits and it is difficult to see any harm in behaving in this way. Equally by never saying no, you are often involved in activities and social outings, which means you don't feel excluded or isolated, which also feels very positive.

WHAT'S BAD ABOUT BEING A SUPERHERO?

Although it can be very rewarding to be a superhero, it does make it very difficult for you to say no or to stop once you are in this role. Also, being a superhero may maintain some dysfunctional assumptions/rules for living as discussed earlier in this book. See the example below that shows how being a superhero may maintain an unhelpful belief and low mood:

As you can see from the cycle above, acting in this way is rewarding, but it can be bad for our confidence and self-esteem. What happens if we cannot help someone or if we don't know how to help them? What we really need to know is whether people will still love us even if we can't help them and/or need to put ourselves first.

Exercise 46

Draw out your own 'superhero' maintenance cycle below and consider what belief this behaviour is maintaining. Then consider how you might change this and monitor your progress.

My superhero maintenance cycle:

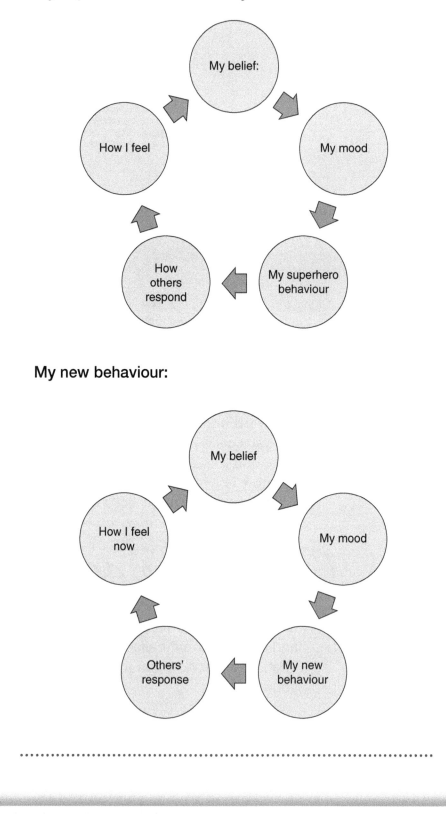

My new behaviour:

This chapter has emphasized the role that maintaining behaviours play in preventing a change in our thoughts, feelings and behaviour. Now that you are aware of these and know how to identify them and the role they play, it is important to continue to try and overcome these and break our unhelpful cycles of behaviour.

Exercise 47

Over the next week identify and change a maintaining behaviour and monitor the impact of this change. Record your experiences so that you may review them at a later date, and to help you monitor changes.

Summary

There are lots of different reasons why people can become angry and why they may behave in an angry way towards someone else. Sometimes people blame their temper and say 'I have a short fuse' or similar, but often the development of anger is more complicated than this.

In certain situations, anger is a very normal and understandable reaction to an event or situation that has occurred, and anger can sometimes pass or dissolve without causing any problems.

Physically, anger is not good for us long term. Often in situations when we are angry we may notice some strong physical reactions.

We start to avoid situations when we feel uncomfortable about them or unable to cope with them in some way. Often with low mood we can avoid situations because we simply don't have the motivation or feel capable of the effort involved. However, avoidance is a classic safety behaviour which actually maintains low mood and anxiety.

Although it can be very rewarding to be a superhero, it does make it very difficult for us to say no or to stop this once we are in this role. Being a superhero may maintain some dysfunctional assumptions/rules for living.

What have I learnt?

→ What behaviours did you identify as relating to your situation? (For example, anger, avoidance, superhero.)

_____

_____

_____

_____

_____

_____

→ What are the good points and bad points that you have noticed about your own behaviour?

_____

_____

_____

_____

_____

_____

→ Why is it important to change some of these behaviours?

_____

_____

_____

_____

_____

_____

→ How would you like to behave in these situations instead?

_____

_____

_____

_____

_____

_____

Where to next?

So far this book has examined many different strategies that you can use to change the way you think, feel and behave. Now it is time to review your goals and monitor progress. The next chapter will talk you through this process and allow you to monitor any changes or progress to date, as well as make a clear plan for the future.

Reviewing your goals

In this chapter you will:

▶ *learn how to break problematic behaviours and maintenance cycles and change your patterns of behaviour.*

▶ *learn to review your goals and consider the impact that some of your changed behaviour has had on your life and what still remains to be acheived.*

▶ *learn to recognize and reward the progress you have made so far.*

What will I have to do?

▶ *You will have to work through and answer the exercises in this chapter, focusing on your own goals and patterns of behaviour and thinking. For 'homework' you will be considering how to take these forward and continue with any progress you have made/ wish to make.*

→ Reviewing your goals

Reviewing our goals is an important part of the CBT process. Not only does it keep us on track and allow us to remember what it is we are trying to achieve, but it also serves to motivate us. If you have reached this chapter and are now considering that you haven't made any changes, and don't feel as though you have achieved any of your original goals, don't despair! Work through Exercise 48, and use the techniques described under the 'Feeling stuck?' section (below) which discusses what happens when we feel stuck and as if we are unable to make changes.

Exercise 48

Reviewing goals and progress worksheet

The goals I originally set myself were: *(List here your original goals set out at the beginning of this process to act as a reminder of what you wanted to achieve)*

_____

_____

_____

_____

In order to complete these goals I have: *(Note down here specific actions that you have completed or challenges that you have undertaken in order to achieve your goal)*

_____

_____

_____

_____

I know I have made changes because now I: *(List here things you have noticed or are doing differently since achieving your goal/started making progress)*

_____

_____

_____

_____

_____

Since completing my goal I have/others have/I feel:
*(List here some of the differences that your goal
has made, either to your own actions/feelings or
perhaps things that other people have noticed/
commented on)*

_____

_____

_____

_____

I have rewarded myself for these goals by: *(List
here the rewards you have treated yourself with for
achieving your goals. If you haven't rewarded yourself
yet then write down how you will reward yourself –
remember: every goal is an achievement no matter
how small)*

_____

_____

_____

_____

_____

These are some goals or challenges which I want to repeat: *(List here any goals that you want to retry or repeat in order to get the most out of them)*

_____

_____

_____

_____

_____

Going forward I want to continue to work on: *(List here remaining goals or further progress that you wish to make)*

_____

_____

_____

_____

_____

→ Feeling stuck?

Looking at the 'Reviewing goals and progress' worksheet in Exercise 48, you may have found it difficult to complete. It may be that when you look at this worksheet, you do not feel that you have made good progress or that you have been able to achieve your goals. This may leave you feeling frustrated and demotivated and you may feel 'stuck' in your current situation. This is a very normal reaction to setting ourselves goals when we feel low or anxious, and we can struggle to recognize our achievements or progress and feel as though nothing has changed. Listed below are some common feelings people have when reviewing goals. Work your way through these sections and the questions that follow – answer these as honestly as you can. *Remember do not criticize or judge yourself*: this is a process and you are not expected to have completed everything by this stage.

→ Common feelings around goal reviewing

'I HAVEN'T ACHIEVED ANYTHING'

Well that just isn't true! For a start, you are on Chapter 11 of this book. So if nothing else, you have managed to persevere and continue reading this book to help you learn strategies to overcome your problems and make progress. If you haven't been able to put these strategies into place yet, then we will consider that at another point, but for now don't dismiss the positive steps that you have made. I once read a wonderful quote which said:

'We will never recognize progress if we continue to look forward at how far we have to go and forget to look backwards and see how far we've come.'

Exercise 49

With that the above quote in mind, consider now the steps you have taken towards overcoming this problem, no matter how small, and list them below:

_____

_____

_____

_____

_____

_____

Remember to reward these small steps towards progress and don't be discouraged – slow progress is still progress, and every small step you take takes you closer to your goal.

'I'VE HAD A REALLY BUSY WEEK/ MONTH/YEAR'

It may be the case that you've been extremely motivated to complete you goals, yet there always seems to be *something* that gets in the way, whether it's other people, work, kids, too many tasks, or unexpected events or people that turn up out of the blue.

Exercise 50

List below everything that you feel has got in the way of you achieving your goals:

_____

_____

_____

_____

_____

Now review the list and ask yourself, which one of these is more important than you? The answer is none. Without making time for ourselves, and by consistently putting ourselves last, we will never build a sense of worth and confidence which will allow us to help ourselves and those around us. If you've ever been on a plane, you'll know in the safety announcement they tell you in the event of a crash, you need to ensure your own safety before helping those around you. This is because unless you look after yourself you will be unable to look after others. The same applies with our mental health. If we do not put ourselves first sometimes we will be unable to help other people.

If putting yourself first is unfamiliar and feels challenging try some of the techniques listed below to help:

1 **Protect your 'me time' as if it were an appointment:** Set aside a time in your week when you can think about you and focus on what you want to achieve. Perhaps think back to your goals to help you decide when is a good time and how much time you need. Write this appointment into your diary or calendar and protect it much as you would a dentist or doctor appointment. When someone asks you for your help, or if something crops up then protect that appointment by explaining you are busy and rearrange. We often put our own needs last and cancel plans for ourselves when we feel needed by other people. However, by protecting the time, you are much more likely to use it and this limits the resentment that we can feel towards other people or things that get in the way of us looking after ourselves. Remember you are worth your own 'me time' and no-one can provide this apart from you.

2 **Be honest about what is needed:** Don't be afraid to tell people that you need 'time out' every now and then. We often mistake putting ourselves first for being selfish. *This is a black and white thinking error* whereby we are either totally available for other people/events or we are selfish. Find some grey area in the middle. It is important that you recognize you need this time and other people need to know that too so that they can also protect that time. Think of other people you know who do things they enjoy – do you think they are 100% selfish? Or are they allowed their 'me time'? If they are allowed, then why aren't you?

3 **Don't say yes when you want to say no:** We know from the previous chapter, which looked at problematic behaviour, that trying to be a superhero and help everyone else, at the expense of our own well-being, simply doesn't work, and leads us to develop and maintain problems. Therefore next time you want to

say 'no', just say it. Don't apologize, or feel you have to offer an excuse, *you are allowed to say no*. It's a small word but very powerful and can mean the difference between you reaching your goal or remaining stuck where you are.

'I'VE TRIED TO GET MOTIVATED BUT JUST CAN'T'

Let's think about what it is you're trying to change/achieve. Look at the questions below and answer them honestly:

1 Is this something you feel you *should* achieve rather than something you *want* to achieve?

2 Are you trying to change/do this for someone else?

3 Do you struggle to see the point of doing this?

4 Do other things feel more important than this?

5 Has someone else suggested you change this/do this?

If the answer to any of the above questions is 'yes' then you need to reconsider what it is that you are trying to achieve. Trying to change something that we don't feel motivated to change is extremely difficult and this can make it harder to stick to and we're more likely to lose interest/not complete the task.

If this is the case, think about why someone else has suggested this, or why something else feels more important. Will doing something else make you happier? If so, then reconsider what it is you are trying to achieve and set yourself new SMART goals (revisit Chapter 4 for goal-setting techniques). You can always come back to this goal, but if you are feeling stuck then changing focus can allow you to make progress in a different area, which in turn will motivate you to come back and challenge this goal, should it still feel important/necessary.

'I'M NOT AS FAR AS I WANTED TO BE AND I AM FEELING REALLY DEMOTIVATED'

This can be a common feeling when we are frustrated by a perceived lack of progress or achievement, or perhaps when we have tried something and 'failed'. Remember the important part to focus on is that you tried/are trying. Even if your progress feels really slow you are still running ahead of all those people that aren't even trying. Try and be kind to yourself and remember why this was important to you in the first place. When you feel like giving up it is important to remember why you started in the first place, and perhaps revisit your cost/benefit analysis for doing this in the first place.

It may be that you need additional support – don't be afraid to ask for help, just make sure you are not avoiding something or getting someone else to do it instead of you, as this will take away from your own sense of achievement. However, if you need some additional support from a friend or family member, then ask them for their help – they may just be able to give you the push you need to take it further, and continue your journey.

Summary

Reviewing our goals is an important part of the CBT process.

Every goal is an achievement no matter how small.

Consider what is standing in your way and change it.

You are allowed to say no.

What have I learnt?

→ Why do you need to review your goals?

_____

_____

_____

_____

_____

_____

→ What is important to remember if you feel 'stuck' in your current situation?

_____

_____

_____

_____

_____

→ What do you need to do if you feel demotivated?

_____

_____

_____

_____

_____

_____

→ How can you protect your 'me time'?

_____

_____

_____

_____

_____

_____

Where to next?

This chapter has focused on reviewing your goals and thinking about some of the issues that may be standing in your way. The next chapter focuses on the future and looks at how to prevent relapses and set-backs.

12 *Avoiding set-backs*

In this chapter you will:
▶ *focus on 'relapse prevention' and on stopping the problem from coming back and getting worse.*
▶ *cement the learning points you have uncovered so far and make a plan for the future to prevent 'relapses'.*
▶ *review the changes you have made and the strategies you have learnt and consider how you will stick with them.*
▶ *learn how to be a 'self-therapist' once you have finished reading this book, and explore what strategies you can put in place to prevent problems from returning and/or worsening.*
▶ *focus on the work you have covered so far and look at planning ahead for the future, so that you can continue to make positive changes.*

What will I have to do?
▶ *You will have to fill in the relapse prevention worksheet which will provide you with a summary of your progress so far and a plan for the future.*

→ How does relapse prevention work?

It is normal in day-to-day life for people to experience low mood or anxiety, as life events happen or situations arise that naturally make us anxious, depressed, angry, stressed or affect our mood in some other way. These are typical reactions to life events and are not something to worry about. However, it is when these moods become more long-term and problematic, or impact on our day-to-day life, that something needs to be done about them. This can be one of the ways that we can distinguish a 'relapse' from a 'normal' reaction to a life event.

In a course of one-to-one therapy, the last couple of sessions would be spent thinking about the skills that you have learnt throughout therapy and focusing on how to continue making positive changes and avoid set-backs in the future. Unless we are working on one very specific goal, it is very unlikely that we will have achieved all the desired goals by the end of therapy. As previously discussed, the aim of CBT is to equip you with skills that you can use whenever and wherever you need to, rather than build a dependence on your therapist or being in therapy in order to make progress.

→ Taking time out for you

By working through this book you will have dedicated some time and energy into focusing on yourself and what you need/want to change for yourself and for your future. It is important that as you finish this book, as you would when finishing therapy, that you continue to spend some time on yourself thinking about what you need and what you want to focus on. It is so easy to get swallowed up in day-to-day life and to put our own needs last or continue to postpone our own happiness or well-being. However ignoring your own needs and putting off making necessary changes is not beneficial and can lead to relapse.

To overcome this, try and commit to a weekly or fortnightly time that you will spend on you, just checking in with yourself about how you are feeling and what you want to achieve.

Exercise 51

Decide on a time that suits you best and put it in your weekly diary/phone calendar to remind you to keep this time for you. To give you some structure for this 'self-therapy' you could try answering the questionnaire below and making any new goals/plans based on your answers.

Weekly check-in questionnaire:

Have I been free from feeling unnecessarily stressed/ anxious/depressed/sad/angry this week?

_____

_____

Was I happy with the way I handled every situation this week?

_____

_____

Have I prioritized my needs this week and put into practice what I have learnt?

_____

_____

Is there anything I would like to do differently over the coming week?

_____

_____

Have I moved closer to achieving my goals?

_____

_____

Have I rewarded any progress I have made?

_____

_____

Have I had a good mix of routine, mastery and pleasurable activities?

_____

_____

If you answered no to any of the above questions then remember, there is no use in self-criticism and there is no space for 'shoulds'. Instead use the plan below to think about the coming week and any changes that you want to put into place for the coming week and how you will change things to move towards your goals and improve your overall well-being.

Over the coming week I would like to:

_____

_____

Break this into a SMART goal using the table below:

Goal	Specific?	Measurable?	Attainable?	Realistic?	Time-limited?	SMART?

My reward for achieving/working towards this goal will be:

_____

_____

_____

_____

I will change a situation next week by using the following techniques that I have learnt:

1 _____

2 _____

3 _____

My next 'self-therapy' appointment will be_____ :

....

Continue to use these worksheets, or adapt them to fit with your own 'self-therapy' sessions each week. The key issue is to keep 'checking in' and making time for yourself to consider your needs and what you are doing and where you want to be going. This will help keep you focused and on-track to achieving what you wish to achieve and making the changes that you wish to make.

Exercise 52

SUMMARY LIST OF ALL KEY STRATEGIES AND CBT SKILLS I HAVE LEARNT THROUGHOUT THIS BOOK

Below is a summary list of the key skills and strategies that you have learnt to use throughout this book. Look at the list and next to the ones that you feel are most relevant to you, write down when and where you might use this strategy. (The aim of this is to give you a quick reference guide to the skills you have learnt and to help you think of when they might be useful to you).

Overview of CBT skills learnt:

Recognizing symptoms of depression and anxiety

_____

_____

_____

_____

Goal-setting

_____

_____

_____

_____

Reframing thoughts

_____

_____

_____

Using the five-area model

_____

_____

_____

Identifying thoughts

_____

_____

_____

Using a thought record

_____

_____

_____

Acting 'as if'

_____

_____

_____

Behavioural experiments

_____

_____

_____

Formulating NATs

_____

_____

_____

Challenging core beliefs

_____

_____

_____

Activity pie charts

_____

_____

_____

Activity scheduling

_____

_____

_____

Identifying thinking errors

_____

_____

_____

Changing behavior

_____

_____

_____

··

→ Focusing on the future

As mentioned above, it is important to spend some time thinking about the future and how you can use your newly learnt skills to prevent situations from reoccurring or falling into old habits of thinking and doing which may result in maintaining a negative mood.

Exercise 53

Take some time to complete the relapse prevention worksheet below. Follow the instructions given underneath each question to help you answer this and form a plan for the future. Remember to acknowledge how far you have come as well as how far you want to get to. Notice any points where you get stuck and come back to them later on.

Relapse Prevention Worksheet

Before I started this process I felt...

(e.g. Include here how you felt when you were facing the problems that this book has helped you with. Try and recall exact emotions or thoughts that you may have experienced. The aim of this is to help you compare where you were and where you are now in your journey's progress.)

_____

_____

_____

_____

Coming towards the end of this book I feel...

(e.g. Make a note here of how you feel given the changes you have made and the strategies you have put in to place. By comparing your before and after experiences you are better able to recognize achievements and changes that otherwise you may take for granted and not reward yourself for.)

_____

_____

_____

_____

I want to continue working towards...

(e.g. Write here what you wish to continue to aim for in the future. Note situations or circumstances in which you would like to be different, and note any particular goals or forthcoming events that you can work towards.)

_____

_____

_____

_____

_____

I know that potential triggers for me feeling *(insert appropriate word for how you have been feeling here e.g. angry/sad/anxious/depressed/stressed, etc.)* are...

(e.g. Note down the potential situations or circumstances that may trigger you feeling this way again in the future, or things that may happen to make you feel worse.)

_____

_____

_____

_____

_____

The strategies I have learnt for dealing with these triggers are...

(e.g. Write down here all the strategies that you have learnt. This should act as a summary list of the strategies you have learnt and how you can use them to tackle this problem.)

_____

_____

_____

_____

_____

Whenever I feel *(insert appropriate word for how you have been feeling here e.g. angry/sad/anxious/ depressed/stressed, etc.)* I will do the following...

(e.g. Use this space to write out a clear plan of what you will do next time you feel this way. For example, your plan may be: (1) step back and consider this from multiple viewpoints; (2) look for the evidence for these thoughts; (3) set a SMART goal to help deal with this situation; (4) decide on a reward and prioritize pleasurable activity. When we feel strong emotions it can be difficult to think logically and rationally; the aim of this section is to create plan you can simply refer rather than trying to remember everything you have learnt when you are feeling upset/angry/depressed, etc.).

_____

_____

_____

_____

_____

My motivation for continuing to work on this is...

(e.g. Think about your end goal(s) and what you want to achieve. Who or what are you doing this for? What will motivate you to keep going when times are tough?)

_____

_____

_____

_____

_____

I know it is important that I...

(e.g. Write down here key lessons that you have learnt. These are not so much specific strategies as more general issues that are important, for example, 'Take time out for myself', 'Ask for help', 'Remember to reward myself for achievements')

_____

_____

_____

_____

_____

In a year I want to be...

(e.g. Imagine yourself a year from now and think what you would like to be doing. Imagine yourself free from any constraints and problems and try and think about where you want to be in a year. The aim of this is to give you a longer-term focus and help you picture the future and what you are aiming for).

_____

_____

_____

_____

_____

In five years I want to be...

(e.g. Similarly to the above question, imagine yourself five years from now and think about what you would like to be doing in five years. Again the aim is to give you focus for the future.)

_____

_____

_____

_____

_____

→ Dealing with relapse

By completing the relapse prevention worksheet you have been able to summarize the skills you have learnt to date and make a plan for the future when you have times of feeling anxious or low in mood. It is important to realize that if a relapse does occur then this does not mean you are back to square one. You can always reapply the techniques as many times as you need to in order to help you achieve what you want and overcome difficult situations.

→ Treat yourself

As well as the therapeutic strategies discussed, it can be helpful to have a few other strategies written down for those days when we feel in need of a boost. When we are feeling low or anxious, it can be hard to think clearly and by having the relapse prevention plan written down, this means we won't get stuck at this point, due to lack of clarity in our thinking. Similarly, it can be useful to write down other strategies that make you feel better and have those to hand.

Exercise 54

Think of all the activities, people and things that make you feel better and write a list below of your top ten:

e.g.

Go for a walk

Watch a funny film

Have a relaxing bath

Etc.

My top ten 'feel-good' strategies are:

1

2

3

4

5

6

7

8

9

10

Again, by not having to think of these in the moment when we may be too tired, stressed or anxious to think clearly, we are allowing ourselves the opportunity to feel better, with very little effort. If you have several things that make you feel better, e.g. a favourite film, then keep these handy so that you have easy access to them and can use them whenever you need to.

By using smaller strategies that give us a boost, we may prevent a situation from getting worse and be able to contain our anxiety and/or low mood until it passes. However, if things do feel as though they are getting worse then you always have your relapse-prevention plan to work with, which will help you. Keep both the plan and your list of treats somewhere obvious so that you have them to hand.

Summary

It is normal in day-to-day life for people to experience low mood or anxiety, as life events happen or situations arise that naturally make us anxious, depressed, angry, stressed or affect our mood in some other way. These are typical reactions to life events and are not something to worry about. However it is when these moods become more long-term and problematic, or impact on our day-to-day life, that something needs to be done about them. This can be one of the ways that we can distinguish a 'relapse' from a 'normal' reaction to a life event.

By working through this book you will have dedicated some time and energy into focusing on yourself and what you need/ want to change for yourself and for your future.

It is important that you continue to spend some time on yourself thinking about what you need and what you want to focus on. It is so easy to get swallowed up in day-to-day life and to put our own needs last or continue to postpone our own happiness or well-being.

However, ignoring your own needs and putting off making necessary changes is not beneficial and can lead to relapse.

What have I learnt?

→ What time is your 'me time' scheduled for in your diary? Why is it important to do this?

_____

_____

_____

_____

_____

_____

→ What are your treats/ favourite rewards for yourself?

_____

_____

_____

_____

_____

_____

→ If you have a relapse, does that mean you are back to square one?

_____

_____

_____

_____

_____

_____

Where to next?

This chapter has focused on summarizing all the skills you have learnt to date and has helped you come up with a clear plan for how you will use them in the future. The next chapters focus on those around you and look at how you can talk to others about the way you have been feeling, and how they can support you.

Introducing people to the new you

In this chapter you will:

▶ *learn to consider those around you and the impact they may be having on your thoughts, feelings, behaviours and physical symptoms.*
▶ *learn to consider the impact that you have on those around you.*
▶ *learn how to explain your goals and achievements to others, and what to do if you come up against unhelpful behaviour from those around you.*

What will I have to do?

▶ *You will have to draw out your 'system' which shows those around you and consider the impact that you have on each other.*
▶ *You will have to complete a worksheet with someone who you would like to talk to about your situation and discuss what you have achieved.*

→ ## I thought this was *my* problem –why do I need to involve other people?

Throughout this book we have explored how our thoughts, feelings and behaviour interact with each other and how this interaction effects what we do, how we feel and how we think. However this interaction goes beyond ourselves and can affect those around us as well. We do not live in isolation but within groups and systems. We may have a group system at work whereby everyone has a different role and interacts with each other according to a hierarchy or their abilities and strengths.

We may also have a system at home, whereby we all have role and act in a certain way or undertake certain tasks because they fit with our role within that particular group. We have previously considered roles in terms of unhelpful behaviours, but we may have other roles to play within our systems. For example, you may be the most organized one within your system who makes sure that things get done. Everyone has a role within many different systems – there is no such thing as living in isolation. Even if you don't live with someone you will still have a role to play in other people's systems and you will impact upon them in some way. If a friend has had a bad day and they come to the pub in a foul mood, it can affect your evening. Maybe they are less talkative or because they are feeling stressed they may drink more and say something they don't mean. Equally when we've had a bad day we may become more irritable and more likely to snap at people or ignore people.

Our behaviour when our mood is affected WILL affect those around us. We can even affect those we don't know by entering their group system and others can affect us. For example, if you get into your car in a foul mood and drive recklessly you may negatively affect other drivers on the road without even meaning to. This is because that bad mood will affect your feelings – you may feel more impatient and more aggressive and therefore drive without your usual care and attention. By looking at these examples it is easy to see that even when we feel totally alone we are actually involved in many different group systems and have a role to play and a way to act within each one.

→ I don't like my role ... can I change it?

Quite often when we make changes in ourselves we realize that we don't like our role within certain systems, or we identify certain aspects of our role that we would like to change. It can feel very difficult to do so. We can feel 'stuck' in our certain role. For example, if you are the one who always organizes everything within your group system, then you may feel stuck in that role because it seems that otherwise nothing would ever get done. However, none of our roles are static – we are not 'stuck' in any of them.

Try and think of our roles as all connected and completely fluid. If one role changes for whatever reason then people around them are able to move and shift in order to accommodate this. Our roles feel stuck because they become habitual and people may meet us whilst we are in one particular role, but there is nothing to stop your role shifting and for them to accommodate that shift – in fact it's healthy. It can be tricky though. If we have felt and acted a certain way for a long time it may mean that people have certain expectations of our behaviour and that they therefore treat us in a certain way. This chapter will help you explain your changing role to others.

→ 'Hi I'm the new me ... Nice to meet you!'

It is important to introduce people to the new you for two main reasons. Firstly, whenever we change something about ourselves we need to strengthen our new behaviour. This prevents us falling back into old habits or behaviours that may have kept a problem going or been unhelpful. It is very easy for us to feel confident on our own about a decision we have made or something new that we want to try out, but sometimes we can lose confidence when we try these new ideas out in front of other people.

By consciously introducing the new you to people you are far more likely to stick to any new plans or changes you have decided upon. It's a very gentle form of peer pressure; once you have told people you are doing something different it is much harder to go back on or not do.

Secondly, some people may have been acting in a way that maintained or possibly even caused the problem to develop in the first place. By introducing them to the new you, you are able to highlight the changes in you and show people how their own behaviour might need to change. People are not psychic and will not automatically know that you feel differently now and so expecting people to 'just know' and react accordingly is unrealistic. We need to hold open and transparent conversations with people in order to make changes last.

→ This is not a blame game

When we talk about the role of other people it is important to realize that this is not a blame game. By that, we mean that it isn't necessarily anyone's fault, including your own, that you ended up in a role in which you feel uncomfortable and which now needs to change. It is easy for others to get into patterns of behaviour that can keep us feeling 'stuck' in a particular role. For example, if you struggle to say no to people and feel people always ask you for help, then they are going to continue to ask you for help because they know you as the person who always says yes and helps. This can make us feel really useful and as though we are being helpful, but we know from previous chapters that it can also make us feel as though we can't say no which is unhelpful.

We need to identify who is around us and the impact we have been having on them and vice versa.

Sit down and plot out all your group systems. Put yourself in the middle and write down all the people who are within your group system, perhaps linking them with yourself as illustrated below:

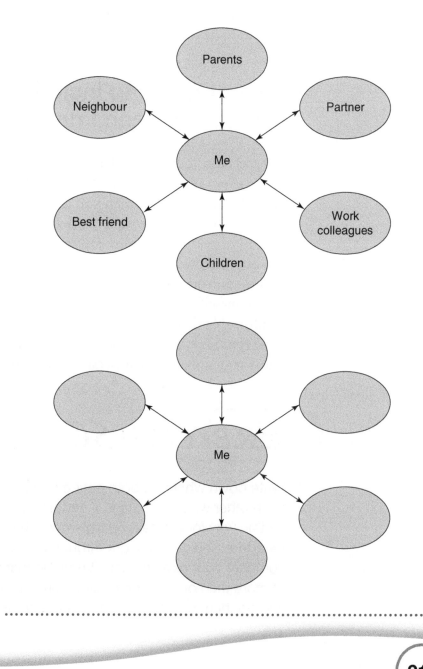

Try then to identify someone in your life who you feel may either have affected or been affected by the problem or situation that you are trying to address. This may be a colleague, a friend, a family member or a partner. They may be involved in one or more of your group systems. Ask your chosen person to make time to sit with you and go through the worksheets and exercises in this chapter. As well as the worksheets here, you will need time and space to work – this is not a conversation to be rushed or fitted in – you both need time to think and reflect and to complete the worksheets.

→ I'm not ready to include anyone else ... what can I do?

If it feels too soon to involve someone else in this process, or if the person you would like to speak to about this is not immediately available, then you can still begin the process without them. Use the same worksheet (Exercise 56) but instead of asking them directly, try to put yourself in their shoes and write a response as though from them, that is, as though from their point of view. Try to be really honest with yourself when completing this worksheet. When it feels comfortable then you can show your chosen person/people how you think your problem affects them and how they affect you and gain their perspective on the situation.

Exercise 56

Write down what you both notice about yourself and each other when you are in a certain situation or feeling a certain way (or whatever problem you have identified to be addressed as you work through this book) and then compare your experiences. It may be that you want to look at more than one feeling or situation which is great, but try and do them one at a time to avoid confusion/ crossover.

When I am (insert situation/feeling here) I notice: When
_____is_____ I notice:

e.g. When I am angry
I notice:

When Lucy is angry I notice:

1. I am irritable
2. I feel less sociable
3. I am tired and tearful
4. You don't hug me

1. She stops going out
2. I have to do more
3. She is a lot more stressed
4. She pushes me away

....

→ # Now what?

Once you have both completed Exercise 56, compare
notes. Remember this isn't about blame or trying to
make someone feel bad – it's just about noticing what
is going on for other people. As with the example given
above, it is likely that what you experience and what
your chosen person experiences are similar and you
may be able to identify links or cross over between your
experiences.

Exercise 57

Once you have identified some of the impact that the
situation is having, it is important to share with your
chosen person what you hope to achieve, or indeed what
you have achieved already through completing this book.
To do this fill in the worksheet below and circle any goals
which you have already completed or started working on,
and then share these with your chosen person.

Worksheet: Sharing my goals

My SMART goals are:

_____

_____

_____

_____

_____

The SMART goal I would like help with is:

_____

_____

_____

_____

_____

Exercise 58

The worksheet below is for you and your chosen person to complete together. First of all share your goals and highlight any goals which you have already started working on/achieved.

The purpose of this worksheet is to help your chosen other identify ways in which they can help support and encourage you to achieve your goals. You can both use the space below to write down some ideas of what they can do to help you.

NB: It is not always easy to ask for help and it can be difficult to accept help when it is offered. Try and complete this exercise as honestly as possible – if something feels uncomfortable ask yourself 'is this maintaining the problem?'. For example, if you feel exhausted all of the time perhaps it is because you find it difficult to ask for help? If you still struggle to complete this exercise honestly then move on to the next worksheet and come back to this exercise later on.

Achieving your goals – how can I help?

In order to achieve my goal of (insert here) I need:

e.g. In order to achieve my goal of leaving the housework to relax more I need:

1 *my partner to help with the house*

2 *to know that it is ok if the house is messy once in a while*

3 *to know when friends are coming over so that I am not caught out if the house is messy*

_____

_____

_____

_____

_____

In order to help (insert here) achieve their goal of (insert here) I need:

e.g. In order to help Lucy achieve her goal of leaving housework to relax more I need:

1 to regularly help with the housework

2 to accept that sometimes the house is going to be messy and that's ok

3 to check Lucy is ok and ask what I can do to help her relax

_____

_____

_____

_____

_____

As you can see there will be some crossover in the help you need and the help your chosen person can offer you. Now go back over the list you have made and rate each of the items in the list according to who is responsible for making sure that item is done. For example, in the example given above Lucy has highlighted that she needs her partner to help more with the housework. However, they identified that Lucy is 50 per cent responsible for this as she needs to highlight what she needs help with. Her partner is 50 per cent responsible for this as he needs to be the one to actually do more, and also Lucy highlighted that it would be good if he could take responsibility for some housework without her asking:

e.g. In order to achieve my goal of leaving the housework to relax more I need:

My partner to help with the housework. This goal is 50% Lucy's responsibility, 50% Lucy's partner's responsibility.

> **Top tip!**
>
> If you and your chosen person cannot agree on whose responsibility a certain task is then try and reach a compromise. For example if you were 100 per cent in charge of housework before and you would like to be 20 per cent in charge of it then how about compromising at 50 per cent and then seeing how you get on?

→ Struggling to complete this worksheet?

Sometimes it is difficult to start the process of asking for help and/or sharing responsibility with your chosen person as there are a number of feelings and emotions that can get in the way of us doing so. Exercise 59 is designed to try and help identify some of the feelings/emotions that are getting in the way of completing the above exercise. Once identified, you will be able to discuss these with your chosen person and can think of ways to overcome these, with a few tips on how to do this provided at the end.

Exercise 59

Both you and your chosen person need to think about how you are both feeling about the situation at the moment. Now look at the list of feelings and emotions below and circle any that feel applicable to you. There may be some crossover or it may be that you are both experiencing completely different emotions at the moment. Either is fine – the important thing is to identify the emotions so that any potential barriers to progress can be highlighted and overcome together.

Circle any emotions that apply to how you are feeling about moving forward with achieving your/their goals and being involved in this process. (NB: You may wish to have a copy each or use different coloured pens to help you identify who is relating to which emotion.)

I feel:

Angry	Resentful
Sad	Worried
Anxious	Depressed
Apprehensive	Overwhelmed
Tearful	Disinterested
Hopeful	Fed-up
Guilty	Responsible
Fearful	Ashamed

Now that you have identified the emotions discuss them together. Include the following questions:

1 Why do I feel like this?

2 Is this feeling getting in the way of helping to achieve my/your goal?

3 How can I change these feelings?

4 How can I feel more positive?

....

Remember: any kind of change can bring about a lot of emotions and it is common to feel a mixture to feelings both positive and negative. What is key is to try and overcome these so they are not acting as a barrier to achieving your goals.

→ I've achieved my goals: I feel great, so why can't they accept the new me?

It can be challenging when we make a positive difference to our own lives and feel as though other people are not supportive or accepting of this change. It is important to remember that people may not mean to be directly critical – they haven't been on the journey you have been on and it may be harder for them to get to grips with the new you and to understand the changes you have made and why. This may mean that people do not act in a way that we would like or that we would expect and this can be difficult to deal with.

However it is important not to let the reactions of others affect the new you – you have worked hard to reach this stage – here's how to overcome this final hurdle and introduce the new you to others:

1 **Be confident.** It can be scary to present a new you to the world and we can feel embarrassed or worry about other people's reactions. Similarly we can worry that other people won't take the new us seriously. The key here is to be confident. If you don't believe in the new you then other people won't either. So be brave and act confidently, even if you don't feel it at first. The more you see how people positively react to the new you the more that confidence will grow until you're not faking it.

2 **Remember your reasons:** And don't be afraid to tell others! Whilst it may not feel comfortable telling them everything you have been doing and learning, it can be helpful to give people an insight. For example, when Jake made a decision to be more boundaried about his working hours and began to leave work on time, a couple of his colleagues made some snide remarks. At first Jake felt bad, but then he remembered how low and

run-down he had been feeling. Next time his colleagues made a comment he said to them, '*I have to leave on time because I realize that I have been spending too much time here and I have been struggling to relax. Knowing I won't still be here at 7 pm has made me much more productive though.*'

3 Don't apologize. You are allowed to make changes and you are allowed to put yourself first. Those around you should understand and support you and if they cannot then it is not your obligation to defend yourself and you should never feel as though you have to apologize for behaving in a way that is protecting your well-being.

Top tip!

Carry this list around with you – in moments when we feel threatened or challenged by other people it can feel harder to stand by decisions we have made. By having this list with you, you will have a constant reminder of why you should be proud of the new you.

Summary

We do not live in isolation but within groups and systems, and everyone has a role within many different systems. Our behaviour WILL affect those around us, whether we mean it to or not.

None of our roles are static; we are not 'stuck' in any of them and other people can shift and change around us.

Whenever we change something about ourselves we need to strengthen our new behaviour. This prevents us falling back into old habits or behaviours that may have kept a problem going or been unhelpful.

By introducing people to the new you, you are able to highlight the changes you have made and the impact this has had on you, as well as show people how their own behaviour might need to change.

When talking about the role of other people it is important to remember that this is not a blame game.

What have I learnt?

→ The key people within my groups or systems are:

_____

_____

_____

_____

_____

_____

→ The three things I need to remember when other people don't accept the 'new me' are:

1 _____

_____

2 _____

_____

3 _____

_____

→The key areas I need other people to understand/help with are:

_____

_____

_____

_____

_____

_____

_____

Where to next?

This chapter has focused on introducing the new you to other people so that they can accept and support the changes that have made or wish to make in the future. The next chapter is aimed at friends, family and carers (FFC) to help them understand more about low mood and anxiety. The aim of the chapter is to provide support and guidance for those living with, or close to, someone with a mental health problem.

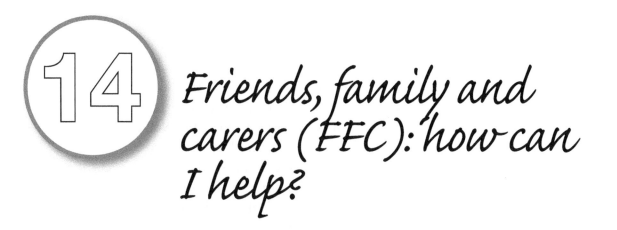

14 Friends, family and carers (FFC): how can I help?

In this chapter you will:
- ▶ *learn how to get guidance and support from those around you.*
- ▶ *learn how to help your FFC gain further understanding into problems that you may be struggling with.*
- ▶ *learn how to deal with and move forward from any difficulties feeling understood and supported.*

What will I have to do?
- ▶ *Introduce this chapter to anyone who you think it could help and let them read through and complete the information and exercises. You don't have to do much in this chapter, but be prepared to have conversations with those around you and answer any questions that they may have as part of their learning process.*

This chapter is not aimed at you but at those around you, so there are no learning aims for you in this chapter. However, for your FFC this chapter will provide some explanations of common problems and the way they may be affecting you, along with helping FFC identify and help with some difficulties that you face. FFC will also be able to identify their own role and see where they can help to support you further.

→ Introduction

As discussed elsewhere in this book, the way we are impacts on those around us, even if we are not deliberately being different. It is important that when we decide to make changes that those around us are aware of what the changes may look like and how they can best support them. This chapter does not exist because FFC are doing anything 'wrong' and this is not a blame game. Rather there is a recognition that the way a person feels and behaves when they are struggling with a mental health problem, no matter how mild, affects those around them and can impact on others' moods and well-being as well. If your friend or partner is feeling particularly low or anxious and you were due to spend the evening together doing something fun, then the likelihood is that their anxiety or depression will impact on the evening. In fact social occasions may even be postponed or cancelled.

This chapter will briefly describe how anxiety and depression work and the impact they may have to help you understand what it is your partner, friend or family member may be going through. The chapter will then look at your own role and how this may be impacting on you.

There will also be a section which looks at some of the common questions and situations that FFC have to face, and will look at how to deal with those situations.

→ What is anxiety?

Anxiety can seem difficult to understand but we all experience anxiety from time to time. Think of the last situation where you felt nervous, scared or uncertain. It is likely that you were experiencing anxiety at this time. There are some common symptoms of anxiety, listed elsewhere in this book, which may help you understand what anxiety feels like and how it can affect people.

HOW DOES IT DEVELOP?

Anxiety can develop for many different reasons. Sometimes it is long-standing anxiety and can be more generalized, for example when people describe themselves as 'naturally anxious' or 'a bit of a worrier'. Other anxieties can develop about very specific situations. For example, someone who is very confident in day-to-day life may feel very anxious about flying on a plane.

WHY ARE THEY ANXIOUS?

In order to answer that question you need to ask the person involved directly. It may be that they don't know why they are anxious, it may be that in certain situations they just feel very anxious. Often with anxiety there can be a 'feared consequence', e.g. a worry that something bad will happen or that something will go wrong. Some people may be reluctant to share this as they may feel 'silly' or foolish in some way. If someone cannot tell you why they are anxious, then they may be able to tell you what that anxiety feels like and when they notice it which is a good start.

→ What is depression?

Depression is also thought of as 'low mood' and this low mood can vary in severity from feeling 'a bit down' which we all experience from time-to-time to something more severe and troubling. The symptoms of depression are listed in Chapter 3.

HOW DOES IT DEVELOP?

As with anxiety, depression may develop around one particular incident or it may have been a long-term feeling that someone has experienced for a long time.

WHY ARE THEY DEPRESSED?

It can be difficult to hear that someone you care about is depressed, especially if they don't seem to have anything to be depressed about. However anyone can get depression – it doesn't matter how wealthy or busy they are, or what positive elements are in their life. Think of depression and anxiety as the 'common cold' of the mind. Anyone can get them at any time, regardless of their situation.

→ Commons questions/situations that FFC face and how to deal with them

There are many common tricky situations that FFC can find themselves facing with no real understanding of how to help or what to do for the best. Below I've listed some of the key questions that I get asked and that FFC tell me they face and I have given a brief answer to these situations below:

WHAT DO I DO WHEN...?

...THEY TELL ME TO 'LEAVE THEM ALONE'

Step one: Don't take it personally. There are many reasons why those with anxiety and depression may ask to be left alone and a lot of them will have nothing to do with your relationship with that person.

The first essential factor is to understand why they are asking to be left alone. With depression it is very common to socially withdraw and not want to see anyone or talk to anyone, no matter who that person is. Equally, with anxiety, people can often feel completely overwhelmed with worry and with anxiety and need to 'retreat' to a place where they don't have to talk to anyone. The same can apply if people are feeling very stressed or angry – there is often a self-preservation attitude of 'just leave me alone!' which doesn't take into account how someone else might feel being told to go away. So step one is don't take it personally.

Step two: Make a judgement call. Only you with knowledge of your relationship will know whether it is best to leave someone to it or whether to ignore this request and try and help. Often it can be a combination of both, giving that person some time and space and then helping them when things feel calmer or less overwhelming for them.

Exercise 60

Look at the questions below and ask your partner/friend/family memeber to fill this in with you and then agree a plan of action for the next time they say 'leave me alone'. Having this plan in place means that you will feel more confident in helping that person and they will feel secure knowing that you know exactly how to look after them when they are feeling this way. Also notice the part about stating how you feel when you are told to go away. It is important to share this as partners and friends may think they are protecting us by telling us to go away as they don't want to burden us, however we can feel rejected and hurt by this behaviour and you need to be able to share this, in a non-blaming way, to help keep an open and honest relationship with that person.

1 Situations when you tell me to 'go away' or shut me out in some way:

(e.g. when you are tearful, when you have had a bad day at work, when you have seen your family)

_____

_____

_____

_____

_____

2 I find it difficult to hear this/do this because:

(e.g. I want to help, I feel shut out, it doesn't feel like the right thing to do)

_____

_____

_____

_____

_____

3 Why do you want to be left alone? (for your partner/ friend/family member to complete):

(e.g. I don't want to burden you/I don't like you seeing me upset/I don't want to talk)

_____

_____

_____

_____

_____

4 What makes you feel better in this situation?

(e.g. I like to go for a walk and then have a relaxing bath)

_____

_____

_____

_____

_____

5 Instead of leaving you alone, next time you feel like this what can I do to help?

(e.g. go for a walk with me and then leave me to have a nice bath whilst you do something else so I don't feel guilty about wasting your time)

_____

_____

_____

_____

_____

6 Next time you feel this way, let's agree that our action plan will be:

(e.g. (1) go for a walk with you; (2) let you have a bath whilst I watch a programme I like; (3) we talk things over when you feel more able)

_____

_____

_____

_____

_____

By having the agreed action plan in place this means that you and your partner/friend know exactly what to do which should help reduce the anxiety and tension around this situation. If the plan doesn't work then go back over it with the person and try and find one that works well for you both. This may involve some trial and error, but ultimately should help you feel calmer and more in control.

...THEY TELL ME I DON'T UNDERSTAND

This can be particularly hurtful to hear, if you feel you do a lot for this person or try and support them as best as you can. One way to tackle this situation is to be open and honest about what your understanding of the situation is and ask them to tell you what is missing/what you have misunderstood. It is very common with anxiety depression and stress, etc. to feel isolated and alone with your problems, which can lead you to believe that no-one understands what you are going through. This may be why your partner, friend or family member tells you that you do not understand.

Exercise 61

Complete the worksheet below and show it to them and ask to have a conversation about what and how they are feeling so that you have a shared understanding:

→ At the moment I think you are feeling _____
  e.g. stressed and anxious

The reason I think this is because I have noticed that you are (write here any symptoms or behaviours that you have noticed)

e.g. tearful, not wanting to go out much, more irritable

_____

_____

_____

_____

_____

My understanding is that you feel this way because
e.g. work

_____

_____

Discussion point: What else do I need to know to understand how you feel? What have I understood correctly? What have I misunderstood?

_____

_____

_____

_____

_____

...THEY ASK ME TO REASSURE THEM OR CHECK THINGS

Reassurance and checking behaviour can make it particularly difficult to know what to do for the best. Often a need for constant reassurance can come from high levels of anxiety whereby people begin to doubt themselves and their decisions and need to seek reassurance from others. When feeling depressed, we can lose confidence in our own beliefs and ideas and seek reassurance from other people as we lose faith in our own judgement.

The hard truth is that reassurance doesn't work. The simple test of this is that if reassurance worked then no one would ever be anxious – it would be as easy as that! If you find you are repeatedly offering reassurance or having to check things for your partner, friend or family member it can be frustrating and time-consuming but also difficult to stop. Often reassurance provides some temporary relief of anxiety and it can make us feel helpful and it seems a relatively simple thing to do to reassure someone and alleviate their anxiety or stress.

However, reassurance in the long term goes against the principles of CBT. If we think back to the earlier CBT principles discussed in this book then we consider the role of evidence and seeking evidence for and against beliefs. If someone asks for reassurance then they are not seeking evidence for or against a belief, they are merely gaging how anxious they should or shouldn't be about a situation.

To give you an example, imagine a child is scared at night and believes that unless their parents tuck them into bed safely and check the wardrobe for monsters then something bad will happen. Whilst it makes sense that all a parent wants to do is reassure their child, by going along with this belief a child never learns that there are no monsters in the wardrobe, and that nothing bad happens if a parent doesn't tuck them in. They are not getting an opportunity to find evidence against their belief. Also, children trust their parents, so if parents go along with this checking then the child may also think 'I am right to be worried, if I was wrong Mum and Dad wouldn't check for me or come and tuck me in'. They may take the reassurance and checking as evidence *for* the idea of monsters existing and something bad happening.

Other issues to consider are whilst this reassurance can seemingly work well in the short term, what happens if you are not there to reassure? Also, others' reassurance-seeking can become invasive and exhausting as well as cause severe disruption to your day. Sometimes an individual will need reassurance at inconvenient times, e.g. the middle of the night, or during your working day, which makes it a further strain on you.

Exercise 62

If you find that you are offering a lot of reassurance to your partner/friend/family member then it is important to look at the CBT and maintenance cycles with them and draw out the role that your reassurance is playing in keeping the problem going. See the example below and then draw out your own cycle in the space provided.

Example maintenance cycle:

Draw your own maintenance cycle(s) in the space below:

...I HATE SEEING THEM UPSET – I JUST WANT TO HELP

Following on from the point above, it can be difficult to know what to do for the best. When someone we care about is distressed it is easy to fall into old habits, such as reassurance giving, simply because we do not know what else to do in that situation. The best way to help your partner/friend/family member is to support the changes they want to make and the goals they want to achieve and be open and honest about what is and isn't helpful for you to do. Consider yourself in this as well. If you run yourself down looking after someone else, you are more likely to suffer from anxiety and/or depression yourself and this will make it harder to help that person anyway.

...I TRY SO HARD BUT THEY STILL CAN'T DO ANYTHING/REFUSE TO SEEK HELP

Although it is frustrating, ultimately it is someone else's decision to seek help. We need to be in the right place in order for to make positive changes in our life. It may be that you bought this book for someone else in order to try and persuade them to consider CBT, or you may have been in contact with mental health services. Ultimately it is the individual's choice and no amount of cajoling can convince someone to seek help if they don't want to. However, do take a look at what you are doing and how you are helping to support this person. If you are keeping them anxiety-free or depression-free enough that they can live their lives normally, but if it feels as though without you things will fall apart, then tell them this. Also the phrase 'cruel to be kind' applies here. Although it can feel really uncomfortable, sometimes you need to stop being so accommodating and 'helpful' as this may actually be preventing someone needing to seek more formal help and ultimately get better in the long term.

Before changing your own behaviour it is important to discuss what you are doing with that person so as to preserve the nature of your relationship.

...I'VE STOPPED BEING THEIR PARTNER/FRIEND AND AM NOW THEIR CARER

If you feel that your role has switched from that of partner, friend or family member and that you now act as a carer for this person, then something needs to change.

...I FEEL OVERWHELMED AND NEED SOME HELP WITH THIS, BUT I DON'T KNOW WHERE TO TURN

It is very common for those who have taken on a 'carer' role to feel overwhelmed and burdened. We can experience all sorts of strong emotions as a carer, including frustration, guilt, sadness, anger and anxiety, all of which will impact on our own well-being. It is very important to look after *yourself* as well as the person you are caring for. There are many charities listed at the back of this book. I would recommend speaking to them as many offer specific support for FFC. Also speak to your GP and make them aware of the situation. Most importantly speak to the person who you are looking after. There is no point pretending the situation is fine if it isn't. By speaking to them they may realize how severe the problem is and what impact that they are having on you. Although it can be difficult, it is important to share this with them, and make a plan for the future. Remember you are not alone in this situation and there are many FFC groups out there that can offer specific support and guidance for your situation.

Summary

It is important that when we decide to make changes, those around us are aware of what the changes may look like and how they can best support them. That is why this chapter exists: this is not a blame game.

It can be difficult to hear that someone you care about is depressed or anxious, especially if they don't seem to have anything to be depressed or anxious about. However anyone can experience depression or anxiety, it doesn't matter what positive elements are in his or her life.

It is very common for those who have taken on a 'carer' role to feel overwhelmed and burdened. We can experience all sorts of strong emotions as a carer including frustration, guilt, sadness, anger and anxiety, all of which will impact on our own well-being.

It is very important to look after **yourself** as well as the person you are caring for.

What have I learnt?

→ Where do you fit into your partner/ friend's maintenance cycle?

_____

_____

_____

_____

_____

_____

→ What can you do to help them?

_____

_____

_____

_____

_____

_____

→What can you do to help yourself?

_____

_____

_____

_____

_____

_____

→Why is it important to look after you and not just the person experiencing the anxiety/ low mood?

_____

_____

_____

_____

_____

_____

→ How will you look after yourself?

_____

_____

_____

_____

_____

_____

_____

Where to next?

This is the final chapter and concludes this introduction to CBT. If you would like further information or wish to seek more advice, please consult the list of helpful numbers and contacts included at the back of this book.

References

Beck, A. (1976) *Cognitive Therapy and the Emotional Disorders*. Oxford, UK: International Universities Press.

Carey, M. and Russell, S. (2002) 'Externalising: Commonly asked questions', *International Journal of Narrative Therapy and Community Work*, 2: 76–84.

Doran, G.T. (1981) 'There's a S.M.A.R.T. way to write management's goals and objectives', *Management Review*, 70, 11: 35–36.

Padesky, C.A. and Mooney, K.A. (1990) 'Clinical Tip: Presenting the cognitive model to clients', *International Cognitive Therapy Newsletter*, 6: 13–14.

Padesky, C.A. (1994) 'Schema change processes in cognitive therapy', *Clinical Psychology & Psychotherapy*, 1, 5: 267–278.

Williams, C. (2001) 'Use of written cognitive behavioural therapy self-help materials to treat depression', *Advances in Psychiatric Treatment*, 7: 233–240.

Wolpe, J. (1958) *Psychotherapy by Reciprocal Inhibition*. Stanford, CA: Stanford University Press.

Appendices

→ ## Appendix A: Five-areas model

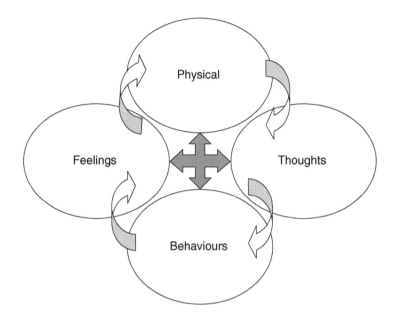

→ Appendix B: Reframing thoughts diary

	Thoughts/feelings I noticed	Reframed thought/feeling
Monday		
Tuesday		
Wednesday		
Thursday		
Friday		
Saturday		
Sunday		

↑ Appendix C: SMART goal worksheet

Goal	Specific?	Measurable?	Attainable?	Realistic?	Time-limited?	SMART?

↑ Appendix D: Five-column thought record

Situation: describe where you were/what you were doing.	Negative Automatic Thoughts (NATs): write down any NATs that popped into your mind during this time. Rate out of 100 how much you believed this thought at the time, with 0 being not at all and 100 being completely.	Feeling: note down how you were feeling in that situation.	Alternative thoughts: write down alternative thoughts that might be relevant in this situation. Rate out of 100 how much you believe this alternative thought, with 0 being not at all and 100 being completely.	How do you feel now?

→ Appendix E: Behavioural experiment worksheet

Date and situation	Key thought being tested/What do you think will happen?	Experiment: What did you do?	What did happen?	How do you feel now?	Re-rated key thought
Write down in detail here when and where you were, who you were with, etc.	*Write down your key cognition/ belief that is going to be tested here. Rate how strongly you believe this thought/belief at the time (%).*	*Write down here what you did to test out the cognition/ test out the belief.*	*Write down here what happened during the experiment*	*Write here how you feel now and anything that you weren't expecting or that surprised you.*	*Re-evaluate that initial key thought/ belief and re-rate how strongly you believe that thought/ belief now (%).*

↑ Appendix F: Seven-column thought record

Situation: describe where you were/ what you were doing.	Negative Automatic Thoughts (NATs): write down any NATs that popped into your mind during this time. Rate out of 100 how much you believed this thought at the time, with 0 being not at all and 100 being completely.	Feeling: note down how you were feeling in that situation.	Evidence to support your negative thought.	Alternative thoughts: write down at least three alternative thoughts that might be relevant in this situation. Rate out of 100 how much you believe this alternative thought, with 0 being not at all and 100 being completely.	Evidence to support your alternative thought.	How do you feel now?

➜ Appendix G: Activity monitoring diary

	Monday	Tuesday	Wednesday	Thursday	Friday	Saturday	Sunday
7.00–8.00 AM							
8.00–9.00							
9.00–10.00							
10.00–11.00							
11.00–12.00							
12.00–1.00 PM							
1.00–2.00							
2.00–3.00							
3.00–4.00							
4.00–5.00							
5.00–6.00							
6.00–7.00							
7.00–8.00							
8.00–9.00							
9.00–10.00							
10.00–11.00							

Useful contacts list

→ **For more information about CBT**

British Association for Behavioural and Cognitive
Psychotherapies

Imperial House

Hornby Street

Bury

Lancashire

BL9 5BN

Tel: 0161 705 4304

Fax: 0161 705 4306

http://www.babcp.com

British Association for Counselling & Psychotherapy

BACP House

15 St John's Business Park

Lutterworth

LE17 4HB

Tel: 01455 883300

Fax: 01455 550243

http://www.bacp.co.uk/

The British Psychological Society

St Andrews House

48 Princess Road East

Leicester

LE1 7DR

Tel: +44 (0)116 254 9568

Fax: +44 (0)116 227 1314

email: enquiries@bps.org.uk

http://www.bps.org.uk

Oxford Cognitive Therapy Centre

Warneford Hospital Oxford

OX3 7JX

Tel: +44 (0)1865 738816

Fax: +44 (0)1865 738817

email: octc@oxfordhealth.nhs.uk

http://www.octc.co.uk

→ Mental health charity websites

http://www.mind.org.uk/

http://www.depressionalliance.org/

http://www.sane.org.uk/

http://www.rethink.org/

http://www.youngminds.org.uk/

http://www.anxietyuk.org.uk/

http://www.ocduk.org/

http://www.nopanic.org.uk/

Index